50 Jewish Holiday Feast Recipes for Home

By: Kelly Johnson

Table of Contents

- Challah Bread
- Matzo Ball Soup
- Gefilte Fish
- Brisket with Tzimmes
- Potato Latkes
- Chicken Soup with Matzo Balls
- Roast Chicken with Herbs
- Kugel (Sweet or Savory)
- Rugelach (Sweet Pastries)
- Charoset (Apple and Nut Salad)
- Honey Cake
- Babka (Sweet Yeast Cake)
- Knishes (Stuffed Dough)
- Chopped Liver
- Blintzes (Cheese or Fruit-filled Crepes)
- Stuffed Cabbage Rolls
- Kreplach (Meat Dumplings)
- Chicken Schnitzel
- Hamentashen (Filled Cookies)
- Sephardic Fish Stew
- Moroccan Carrot Salad
- Israeli Couscous Salad
- Pomegranate Chicken
- Lamb Tagine
- Spinach Borekas
- Shakshuka
- Halva (Sesame Sweet)
- Falafel with Tahini Sauce
- Jerusalem Bagels
- Sabich (Eggplant Sandwich)
- Tahini Cookies
- Yemenite Soup
- Turkish Delight
- Sufganiyot (Jelly Donuts)
- Lemon Garlic Hummus

- Israeli Salad
- Persian Rice Pilaf
- Stuffed Grape Leaves (Dolmas)
- Honey Roasted Vegetables
- Chocolate Babka
- Coconut Macaroons
- Israeli Shakshuka
- Chicken with Preserved Lemons
- Yemenite Kubaneh Bread
- Date Charoset Truffles
- Cheese Burekas
- Beet Salad with Goat Cheese
- Apple Kugel
- Turkish Coffee
- Fruit Compote

Challah Bread

Ingredients:

- 4 cups all-purpose flour
- 1/4 cup granulated sugar
- 1 packet (2 1/4 tsp) active dry yeast
- 1 1/4 tsp salt
- 2/3 cup lukewarm water
- 1/4 cup vegetable oil
- 2 large eggs, plus 1 egg for egg wash
- Sesame seeds or poppy seeds (optional, for topping)

Instructions:

In a large mixing bowl, combine 3 cups of flour, sugar, yeast, and salt.
In a separate bowl, whisk together the lukewarm water, vegetable oil, and 2 eggs.
Make a well in the center of the dry ingredients and pour in the wet ingredients.
Mix with a spoon until the dough starts to come together.
Turn the dough out onto a floured surface. Knead the dough for about 8-10 minutes, adding more flour as needed, until you have a smooth and elastic dough.
Place the dough in a greased bowl and cover with a clean kitchen towel. Let it rise in a warm place for about 1-1.5 hours, or until doubled in size.
After the dough has risen, punch it down to release the air. Divide the dough into 3 equal portions.
Roll each portion into a long rope, about 16-18 inches long.
Pinch together one end of the ropes and then braid them together. Pinch the other end together and tuck both ends under the loaf.
Place the braided loaf on a parchment-lined baking sheet. Cover with a towel and let it rise again for about 30-45 minutes.
Preheat your oven to 350°F (175°C).
Beat the remaining egg and brush it over the risen challah. Sprinkle with sesame seeds or poppy seeds if desired.
Bake the challah in the preheated oven for 25-30 minutes or until golden brown and the bottom sounds hollow when tapped.
Let the challah cool on a wire rack before slicing and serving.

Enjoy your homemade Challah bread!

Matzo Ball Soup

Ingredients:

For the Matzo Balls:

- 4 large eggs
- 1/4 cup vegetable oil
- 1 cup matzo meal
- 1 teaspoon salt
- 4 tablespoons chicken broth or water
- 1/4 teaspoon black pepper
- 1/4 teaspoon garlic powder (optional)

For the Soup:

- 2 tablespoons vegetable oil
- 1 onion, finely chopped
- 2 carrots, peeled and sliced
- 2 celery stalks, sliced
- 2 cloves garlic, minced
- 8 cups chicken broth
- Salt and pepper, to taste
- Fresh dill or parsley, chopped (for garnish)

Instructions:

Prepare the Matzo Balls:
- In a large mixing bowl, beat the eggs with vegetable oil until well combined.
- Add matzo meal, salt, black pepper, garlic powder (if using), and chicken broth or water. Mix until a uniform batter forms.
- Cover the bowl and refrigerate for at least 30 minutes (or up to 2 hours) to firm up the mixture.

Form the Matzo Balls:

- After chilling, wet your hands with cold water and shape the matzo mixture into 1-inch balls (about the size of a walnut). Wet hands periodically to prevent sticking.
- Place the formed matzo balls on a plate or baking sheet. You should get around 12-15 matzo balls.

Cook the Matzo Balls:
- In a large pot, bring salted water to a boil.
- Carefully drop the matzo balls into the boiling water.
- Reduce heat to a simmer, cover the pot, and cook for about 20-30 minutes or until the matzo balls are tender and cooked through.
- Remove the cooked matzo balls from the water using a slotted spoon and set aside.

Prepare the Soup:
- In another large pot, heat vegetable oil over medium heat.
- Add chopped onion, carrots, and celery. Sauté for 5-7 minutes until vegetables begin to soften.
- Add minced garlic and sauté for another 1-2 minutes until fragrant.

Combine Soup and Matzo Balls:
- Pour in chicken broth into the pot with the sautéed vegetables.
- Bring the soup to a simmer. Season with salt and pepper to taste.
- Carefully add the cooked matzo balls into the simmering soup.

Serve:
- Let the soup simmer for a few more minutes to heat the matzo balls through.
- Ladle the hot soup into bowls.
- Garnish with chopped fresh dill or parsley.
- Serve hot and enjoy your comforting Matzo Ball Soup!

This recipe serves about 6-8 servings. It's perfect for a cozy meal, especially during Jewish holidays like Passover.

Gefilte Fish

Ingredients:

For the Fish:

- 1 pound boneless, skinless white fish fillets (such as carp, pike, or whitefish)
- 1/2 pound boneless, skinless fish fillets (such as salmon or trout)
- 2 onions, finely chopped
- 2 eggs
- 1/4 cup matzo meal or breadcrumbs
- 2 teaspoons salt
- 1/2 teaspoon black pepper
- 2 tablespoons sugar
- Ice water, as needed

For the Broth:

- 2 carrots, peeled and sliced
- 1 onion, sliced
- 2 celery stalks, sliced
- 1 bay leaf
- 8 cups fish stock or water
- 1/4 cup sugar
- 1/4 cup white vinegar
- Salt and pepper, to taste
- Fresh dill, for garnish

Instructions:

Prepare the Fish Mixture:
- In a food processor, combine the white fish fillets, salmon (or trout) fillets, and chopped onions. Pulse until finely ground.
- Transfer the ground fish mixture to a large mixing bowl.
- Add eggs, matzo meal (or breadcrumbs), salt, pepper, and sugar to the bowl.

- Mix everything together until well combined. The mixture should be thick and sticky. If too dry, gradually add ice water, 1 tablespoon at a time, until the desired consistency is reached.

Shape the Gefilte Fish:
- Wet your hands with cold water to prevent sticking.
- Scoop up about 2 tablespoons of fish mixture and shape it into an oval-shaped patty or ball. Repeat with the remaining mixture.
- Place the formed fish patties/balls on a plate or baking sheet lined with parchment paper.

Prepare the Broth:
- In a large pot, combine carrots, sliced onion, celery, bay leaf, fish stock (or water), sugar, and vinegar.
- Season with salt and pepper to taste.
- Bring the broth to a simmer over medium heat.

Cook the Gefilte Fish:
- Carefully add the shaped fish patties/balls into the simmering broth.
- Cover the pot partially with a lid and simmer gently for about 45-60 minutes, stirring occasionally, until the gefilte fish is cooked through and firm.

Chill and Serve:
- Remove the pot from heat and let the gefilte fish cool in the broth.
- Once cooled, transfer the gefilte fish patties/balls along with some of the broth to a serving dish.
- Cover and refrigerate until ready to serve.

Serve Gefilte Fish:
- Serve gefilte fish chilled, garnished with fresh dill.
- Serve with horseradish or beet horseradish on the side, if desired.

Enjoy this homemade gefilte fish as a traditional appetizer or side dish during Jewish holiday feasts, especially on Passover!

Brisket with Tzimmes

Ingredients:

- 3-4 pounds beef brisket
- Salt and black pepper, to taste
- 2 tablespoons vegetable oil
- 2 onions, thinly sliced
- 4 cloves garlic, minced
- 4 cups beef broth or chicken broth
- 1 cup dry red wine (optional)
- 1 tablespoon tomato paste
- 1 tablespoon honey
- 1 tablespoon Dijon mustard
- 1 teaspoon paprika
- 1/2 teaspoon dried thyme
- 1/2 teaspoon dried rosemary
- 1 pound carrots, peeled and cut into chunks
- 1 pound sweet potatoes, peeled and cut into chunks
- 1 pound prunes, pitted
- 1/2 cup dried apricots
- Salt and pepper, to taste
- Chopped fresh parsley, for garnish

Instructions:

Preheat and Season:
- Preheat your oven to 325°F (160°C).
- Season the brisket generously with salt and black pepper on both sides.

Sear the Brisket:
- In a large Dutch oven or heavy-bottomed pot, heat vegetable oil over medium-high heat.
- Sear the brisket for about 4-5 minutes on each side until browned. Remove the brisket from the pot and set aside.

Saute Onions and Garlic:
- In the same pot, add sliced onions and minced garlic. Saute for 3-4 minutes until onions are softened and translucent.

Deglaze and Add Flavorings:

- Pour in the beef broth (or chicken broth) and red wine (if using), scraping up any browned bits from the bottom of the pot.
- Stir in tomato paste, honey, Dijon mustard, paprika, dried thyme, and dried rosemary. Mix well to combine.

Add Brisket Back and Simmer:
- Return the seared brisket back into the pot, along with any juices.
- Bring the liquid to a simmer, then cover the pot with a lid.
- Transfer the pot to the preheated oven and braise for about 2.5 to 3 hours, or until the brisket is tender and can be easily pierced with a fork.

Prepare the Tzimmes:
- In a large bowl, combine carrots, sweet potatoes, prunes, and dried apricots.
- After the brisket has cooked for about 2 hours, add the mixed vegetables and fruits around the brisket in the pot.
- Cover the pot again and continue to braise for another 30-60 minutes until the vegetables are tender and the brisket is fully cooked.

Serve:
- Carefully remove the brisket from the pot and transfer it to a cutting board.
- Let the brisket rest for a few minutes, then slice it against the grain into thick slices.
- Arrange the sliced brisket on a serving platter, surrounded by the tzimmes (vegetables and fruits).
- Season the tzimmes with salt and pepper to taste.
- Garnish with chopped fresh parsley before serving.

Enjoy this delicious Brisket with Tzimmes as a main course for your Jewish holiday feast. The sweet and savory flavors will surely delight your guests!

Potato Latkes

Ingredients:

- 4 large potatoes (Russet or Yukon Gold), peeled
- 1 onion, peeled
- 2 large eggs, beaten
- 3 tablespoons all-purpose flour or matzo meal
- 1 teaspoon salt, or to taste
- 1/2 teaspoon black pepper
- Vegetable oil, for frying
- Applesauce and sour cream, for serving (optional)

Instructions:

Grate Potatoes and Onion:
- Use a box grater or a food processor with a grating attachment to grate the potatoes and onion.
- Place the grated potatoes and onion in a clean kitchen towel or cheesecloth. Squeeze out as much liquid as possible over the sink.

Mix the Latke Batter:
- In a large mixing bowl, combine the grated and drained potatoes and onion.
- Add beaten eggs, flour or matzo meal, salt, and black pepper. Mix everything together until well combined.

Heat the Oil:
- In a large skillet or frying pan, heat about 1/4 inch of vegetable oil over medium-high heat until hot but not smoking. Use enough oil to generously coat the bottom of the pan.

Form and Fry the Latkes:
- Take a heaping tablespoon of the potato mixture and gently drop it into the hot oil, flattening it slightly with a spatula to form a pancake shape.
- Continue forming latkes and carefully place them in the hot oil, making sure not to overcrowd the pan. Leave space between each latke for easy flipping.

Fry Until Golden Brown:

- Fry the latkes for about 3-4 minutes on each side, or until golden brown and crispy. Use a spatula to carefully flip the latkes halfway through cooking.

Drain and Keep Warm:
- Once done, transfer the cooked latkes to a plate lined with paper towels to drain excess oil. Keep the latkes warm in a low oven (about 200°F or 95°C) while you finish frying the remaining batches.

Serve and Enjoy:
- Serve the potato latkes hot with applesauce and sour cream on the side, if desired.
- Enjoy these crispy and delicious potato latkes as a festive appetizer or side dish during your Jewish holiday feast, especially for Hanukkah!

Tip: For variation, you can add grated carrots or zucchini to the latke mixture for extra flavor and color. Experiment with different toppings like smoked salmon, herbed cream cheese, or even caviar for a gourmet twist.

Chicken Soup with Matzo Balls

For the Chicken Soup:

Ingredients:

- 1 whole chicken (about 3-4 pounds), cut into pieces
- 2 onions, peeled and halved
- 4 carrots, peeled and cut into chunks
- 4 celery stalks, cut into chunks
- 2 parsnips, peeled and cut into chunks (optional)
- 1 bunch fresh dill
- 1 bunch fresh parsley
- Salt and black pepper, to taste
- Water, to cover

Instructions:

Prepare the Chicken Broth:
- In a large soup pot, place the chicken pieces (including bones) and cover with cold water.
- Add the halved onions, carrots, celery, parsnips (if using), and a bunch of fresh dill and parsley to the pot.
- Season with salt and black pepper.

Simmer the Soup:
- Bring the pot to a boil over medium-high heat, skimming off any foam that rises to the surface.
- Reduce the heat to low, cover the pot partially with a lid, and let the soup simmer gently for about 2-3 hours. The longer you simmer, the richer the flavor will be.

Strain the Broth:
- Once the soup has simmered and the chicken is tender, remove the chicken pieces and vegetables from the pot using a slotted spoon.
- Strain the broth through a fine-mesh sieve or cheesecloth into another large pot or bowl. Discard the solids.

Shred the Chicken:
- Allow the chicken pieces to cool slightly, then shred the meat into bite-sized pieces using forks or your hands. Discard the bones and skin.

For the Matzo Balls:

Ingredients:

- 4 large eggs
- 1/4 cup chicken fat (schmaltz) or vegetable oil
- 1 cup matzo meal
- 1 teaspoon salt
- 1/4 teaspoon black pepper
- 4 tablespoons chicken broth or water

Instructions:

Prepare the Matzo Ball Mixture:
- In a large mixing bowl, whisk together the eggs and chicken fat (or vegetable oil) until well combined.
- Stir in the matzo meal, salt, black pepper, and chicken broth (or water) until a sticky dough forms.
- Cover the bowl and refrigerate the mixture for at least 30 minutes (or up to 2 hours) to firm up.

Form the Matzo Balls:
- After chilling, wet your hands with cold water and shape the matzo mixture into small balls, about 1 inch in diameter. Wet hands periodically to prevent sticking.
- Place the formed matzo balls on a plate or baking sheet.

Cook the Matzo Balls:
- In a large pot of boiling salted water, drop the matzo balls carefully.
- Reduce the heat to a simmer, cover the pot with a lid, and cook the matzo balls for about 30-40 minutes until they are cooked through and fluffy. They will float to the surface when done.

To Serve:

Assemble the Soup:
- Return the strained chicken broth to the pot and bring it back to a simmer.
- Add the shredded chicken back into the pot to heat through.
- Carefully add the cooked matzo balls to the hot soup.

Serve Warm:
- Ladle the Chicken Soup with Matzo Balls into bowls.
- Garnish with freshly chopped dill or parsley, if desired.
- Serve hot and enjoy this comforting and flavorful dish during your Jewish holiday feast or any time you crave a hearty bowl of soup!

Roast Chicken with Herbs

Ingredients:

- 1 whole chicken (about 4-5 pounds), giblets removed
- Salt and black pepper, to taste
- 2 tablespoons olive oil or melted butter
- 2 cloves garlic, minced
- 1 tablespoon fresh rosemary, chopped
- 1 tablespoon fresh thyme leaves
- 1 tablespoon fresh parsley, chopped
- 1 lemon, halved
- Additional fresh herbs for garnish (optional)

Instructions:

Preheat the Oven:
- Preheat your oven to 425°F (220°C) and position the rack in the middle.

Prepare the Chicken:
- Pat the chicken dry with paper towels. This helps to ensure crispy skin during roasting.
- Season the chicken generously inside and out with salt and black pepper.

Herb and Garlic Rub:
- In a small bowl, mix together the olive oil (or melted butter), minced garlic, chopped rosemary, thyme, and parsley to make an herb rub.
- Rub the herb mixture all over the outside of the chicken, making sure to coat it evenly.

Stuff the Chicken:
- Place the lemon halves inside the cavity of the chicken. This will help to infuse the chicken with citrus flavor while roasting.

Tie the Chicken (Optional):
- If desired, tie the legs of the chicken together with kitchen twine. This helps the chicken to roast evenly.

Roast the Chicken:
- Place the seasoned and stuffed chicken on a roasting pan or baking dish, breast side up.

- Roast the chicken in the preheated oven for about 1 hour to 1 hour and 15 minutes, or until the skin is golden brown and crispy, and the internal temperature of the thickest part of the thigh reaches 165°F (75°C).

Rest and Serve:
- Once the chicken is cooked through, remove it from the oven and let it rest for about 10-15 minutes before carving.
- Tent the chicken loosely with foil to keep it warm during resting.
- Carve the roast chicken into serving pieces.
- Garnish with additional fresh herbs, if desired.
- Serve the roast chicken with your favorite side dishes, such as roasted vegetables, mashed potatoes, or a fresh salad.

Enjoy this delicious and aromatic roast chicken with herbs as the centerpiece of your Jewish holiday feast. The combination of garlic, rosemary, thyme, and lemon will elevate the flavors of the tender and juicy chicken!

Kugel (Sweet or Savory)

Ingredients:

- 8 ounces wide egg noodles
- 4 large eggs
- 1/2 cup unsalted butter, melted
- 1 cup sour cream
- 1 cup cottage cheese
- 1 cup whole milk
- 3/4 cup granulated sugar
- 1 teaspoon vanilla extract
- 1/2 teaspoon ground cinnamon
- 1/4 teaspoon salt
- 1 cup golden raisins (optional)
- 1/2 cup cornflake crumbs or breadcrumbs
- Additional cinnamon and sugar for sprinkling

Instructions:

Preheat the Oven:
- Preheat your oven to 350°F (175°C). Grease a 9x13-inch baking dish.

Cook the Noodles:
- Cook the egg noodles according to package instructions until al dente. Drain and set aside.

Prepare the Custard Mixture:
- In a large bowl, whisk together the eggs, melted butter, sour cream, cottage cheese, milk, sugar, vanilla extract, cinnamon, and salt until smooth.

Combine and Bake:
- Add the cooked and drained noodles to the custard mixture. Stir in the golden raisins if using.
- Pour the noodle mixture into the prepared baking dish.
- In a small bowl, mix together the cornflake crumbs (or breadcrumbs) with a sprinkle of cinnamon and sugar. Sprinkle this mixture evenly over the top of the kugel.

Bake the Kugel:

- Bake in the preheated oven for 45-55 minutes, or until the kugel is set and the top is golden brown.

Serve:
- Let the kugel cool slightly before serving.
- Cut into squares and serve warm or at room temperature. Enjoy this sweet and comforting kugel as a side dish or dessert.

Savory Kugel (Potato Kugel)

Ingredients:

- 6 large potatoes, peeled
- 2 onions
- 4 large eggs
- 1/2 cup matzo meal or breadcrumbs
- 1/4 cup vegetable oil
- 2 teaspoons salt
- 1/2 teaspoon black pepper
- 1/2 teaspoon garlic powder
- Chopped fresh parsley or dill (optional, for garnish)

Instructions:

Preheat the Oven:
- Preheat your oven to 375°F (190°C). Grease a 9x13-inch baking dish.

Grate Potatoes and Onions:
- Grate the peeled potatoes and onions using a box grater or food processor.

Combine Ingredients:
- In a large bowl, beat the eggs. Add the grated potatoes and onions, matzo meal (or breadcrumbs), vegetable oil, salt, pepper, and garlic powder. Mix well to combine.

Bake the Kugel:
- Pour the potato mixture into the prepared baking dish, spreading it out evenly.
- Bake in the preheated oven for about 1 hour to 1 hour and 15 minutes, or until the top is golden brown and crispy.

Serve:
- Let the potato kugel cool slightly before serving.
- Cut into squares and garnish with chopped fresh parsley or dill, if desired.
- Serve warm as a delicious and savory side dish for your holiday feast.

Enjoy making and serving these classic kugel recipes—whether sweet or savory—for a memorable addition to your Jewish holiday table!

Rugelach (Sweet Pastries)

Ingredients:

For the Dough:

- 1 cup unsalted butter, softened
- 8 ounces cream cheese, softened
- 1/4 cup granulated sugar
- 1/4 teaspoon salt
- 2 cups all-purpose flour

For the Filling:

- 1/2 cup apricot preserves or raspberry jam
- 1/2 cup brown sugar
- 1 tablespoon ground cinnamon
- 1 cup finely chopped nuts (walnuts, pecans, or almonds)
- 1/2 cup raisins or currants (optional)
- 1/2 cup mini chocolate chips (optional)

For Assembly and Topping:

- 1 egg, beaten (for egg wash)
- Granulated sugar or coarse sugar (for sprinkling)

Instructions:

Prepare the Dough:
- In a large bowl or using a stand mixer, beat together the softened butter, cream cheese, sugar, and salt until smooth and creamy.
- Gradually add the flour, mixing until the dough comes together and forms a ball.
- Divide the dough into 4 equal portions, shape each portion into a disc, wrap in plastic wrap, and refrigerate for at least 1 hour (or overnight) until firm.

Make the Filling:

- In a small bowl, mix together the apricot preserves (or jam), brown sugar, cinnamon, chopped nuts, raisins or currants (if using), and mini chocolate chips (if using). Set aside.

Assemble the Rugelach:
- Preheat your oven to 350°F (175°C). Line baking sheets with parchment paper.
- Take one disc of dough out of the refrigerator at a time.
- On a lightly floured surface, roll out the dough into a circle about 1/8-inch thick.
- Spread a thin layer of the filling mixture evenly over the dough circle, leaving a small border around the edges.
- Using a pizza cutter or sharp knife, cut the dough circle into 12 equal wedges (like slicing a pizza).

Roll and Shape the Rugelach:
- Starting from the wide end, roll up each wedge of dough to form a crescent shape.
- Place the rugelach, point side down, on the prepared baking sheets, spacing them slightly apart.

Brush with Egg Wash and Sprinkle with Sugar:
- Brush the tops of the rugelach with beaten egg (egg wash).
- Sprinkle each rugelach with a little granulated sugar or coarse sugar for a sweet, crunchy topping.

Bake the Rugelach:
- Bake in the preheated oven for 20-25 minutes, or until golden brown and flaky.
- Remove from the oven and let cool on the baking sheets for a few minutes before transferring to a wire rack to cool completely.

Serve and Enjoy:
- Store the cooled rugelach in an airtight container at room temperature.
- Enjoy these delicious, flaky rugelach as a sweet treat for your Jewish holiday feast or any time you crave a delightful pastry!

Feel free to customize the filling with your favorite ingredients and flavors. Rugelach are best enjoyed fresh but can also be frozen for longer storage. Enjoy baking and sharing these delightful sweet pastries!

Charoset (Apple and Nut Salad)

Ingredients:

- 3 medium apples, peeled, cored, and finely chopped (use a mix of sweet and tart apples like Granny Smith and Honeycrisp)
- 1 cup chopped walnuts or pecans
- 1/2 cup sweet red wine (such as Manischewitz)
- 1 teaspoon ground cinnamon
- 2-3 tablespoons honey, to taste

Instructions:

Prepare the Apples and Nuts:
- Finely chop the peeled, cored apples into small pieces. You can use a food processor for a quicker chop, but be careful not to over-process.
- Chop the walnuts or pecans into small pieces. You can toast them lightly in a dry skillet over medium heat for extra flavor, if desired.

Combine Ingredients:
- In a mixing bowl, combine the chopped apples and nuts.
- Add the sweet red wine, ground cinnamon, and honey to the bowl.

Mix Thoroughly:
- Mix all the ingredients together until well combined. The mixture should be moist but not too liquidy.

Adjust to Taste:
- Taste the Charoset and adjust the sweetness by adding more honey, if desired.
- You can also add more cinnamon or wine based on your personal preference.

Chill Before Serving:
- Cover the Charoset mixture and refrigerate for at least 1 hour (or overnight) before serving. This allows the flavors to meld together.

Serve:
- Before serving, give the Charoset a final stir.
- Serve the Charoset as part of the Passover Seder meal, traditionally eaten with matzo as a symbolic reminder of the mortar used by the Israelites.

Variations:

- Some recipes may include additional ingredients such as chopped dates, figs, or raisins for added sweetness and texture.
- Adjust the consistency of the Charoset by adding more wine or honey, depending on your preference.
- Experiment with different types of apples and nuts to create your own unique version of Charoset.

Enjoy this classic Charoset recipe during Passover or as a delicious apple and nut salad any time of the year!

Honey Cake

Ingredients:

- 3 cups all-purpose flour
- 1 tablespoon baking powder
- 1 teaspoon baking soda
- 1/2 teaspoon salt
- 1 tablespoon ground cinnamon
- 1/2 teaspoon ground cloves
- 1/2 teaspoon ground allspice
- 1 cup vegetable oil
- 1 cup honey
- 1 1/2 cups granulated sugar
- 1/2 cup brown sugar
- 3 large eggs
- 1 teaspoon vanilla extract
- 1 cup warm coffee or strong tea
- 1/2 cup orange juice
- Zest of 1 orange

For Garnish (optional):

- Powdered sugar, for dusting
- Sliced almonds or chopped walnuts, for topping

Instructions:

Preheat the Oven and Prepare the Pan:
- Preheat your oven to 350°F (175°C). Grease and flour a 9x13-inch baking pan or two 9-inch round cake pans.

Combine Dry Ingredients:
- In a large bowl, whisk together the flour, baking powder, baking soda, salt, cinnamon, cloves, and allspice. Set aside.

Mix Wet Ingredients:
- In another large bowl, whisk together the vegetable oil, honey, granulated sugar, brown sugar, eggs, and vanilla extract until well combined.

Combine Wet and Dry Mixtures:

- Gradually add the dry ingredients to the wet ingredients, alternating with the warm coffee (or tea) and orange juice, mixing until just combined. Be careful not to overmix.

Add Orange Zest:
- Fold in the orange zest into the batter until evenly distributed.

Bake the Cake:
- Pour the batter into the prepared baking pan(s), spreading it out evenly.
- Bake in the preheated oven for 45-55 minutes, or until a toothpick inserted into the center of the cake comes out clean.

Cool and Serve:
- Allow the cake to cool in the pan for about 15 minutes, then transfer to a wire rack to cool completely.
- Once cooled, dust the top of the cake with powdered sugar and sprinkle with sliced almonds or chopped walnuts, if desired.

Serve and Enjoy:
- Slice and serve the honey cake as a sweet and festive dessert for Rosh Hashanah or any special occasion.
- Store any leftovers in an airtight container at room temperature for up to 3-4 days, or freeze for longer storage.

This honey cake is perfect for celebrating Jewish holidays or for sharing with family and friends. The combination of honey, spices, and orange zest creates a rich and flavorful cake that everyone will love!

Babka (Sweet Yeast Cake)

Ingredients:

For the Dough:

- 4 cups all-purpose flour
- 1/2 cup granulated sugar
- 2 1/4 teaspoons (1 packet) active dry yeast
- 1 teaspoon salt
- 3/4 cup warm milk (about 110°F or 43°C)
- 2 large eggs, room temperature
- 1 teaspoon vanilla extract
- 1/2 cup unsalted butter, softened

For the Chocolate Filling:

- 8 ounces semi-sweet or bittersweet chocolate, finely chopped
- 1/2 cup unsalted butter
- 1/2 cup granulated sugar
- 1 tablespoon ground cinnamon

For the Syrup (Optional):

- 1/2 cup water
- 1/2 cup granulated sugar

Instructions:

Prepare the Dough:
- In a large mixing bowl or the bowl of a stand mixer, combine 3 cups of flour, sugar, yeast, and salt.
- Add warm milk, eggs, and vanilla extract. Mix until well combined.
- Gradually add the softened butter, mixing until the dough comes together.
- Gradually add the remaining 1 cup of flour, a little at a time, until the dough is smooth and slightly sticky.

Knead the Dough:

- Turn the dough out onto a lightly floured surface. Knead the dough for about 5-8 minutes until smooth and elastic. Alternatively, use a stand mixer with a dough hook attachment to knead the dough.

First Rise:
- Place the dough in a greased bowl, turning to coat all sides of the dough with oil.
- Cover with plastic wrap or a clean kitchen towel and let it rise in a warm place until doubled in size, about 1-2 hours.

Prepare the Chocolate Filling:
- In a heatproof bowl, combine chopped chocolate, butter, sugar, and ground cinnamon.
- Microwave in short intervals or use a double boiler to melt the mixture until smooth. Set aside to cool slightly.

Assemble the Babka:
- Punch down the risen dough and divide it into two equal portions.
- Roll out each portion into a rectangle (about 12x16 inches) on a lightly floured surface.
- Spread half of the chocolate filling evenly over each rectangle, leaving a small border around the edges.

Roll and Twist:
- Starting from one long side, tightly roll up the dough into a log.
- Use a sharp knife to cut the log in half lengthwise, exposing the layers of filling.
- Twist the two halves together, keeping the cut sides facing up.

Second Rise and Bake:
- Place each twisted dough into a greased loaf pan or on a baking sheet lined with parchment paper.
- Cover loosely with plastic wrap or a kitchen towel and let it rise again for about 1 hour until puffy.

Preheat and Bake:
- Preheat your oven to 350°F (175°C).
- Bake the babkas for 25-30 minutes, or until golden brown and cooked through.

Make Syrup (Optional):
- In a small saucepan, combine water and sugar. Bring to a simmer over medium heat, stirring until sugar is dissolved.
- Brush the warm syrup over the hot babkas as soon as they come out of the oven.

Cool and Serve:

- Let the babkas cool in the pans for about 10 minutes, then transfer to a wire rack to cool completely.
- Slice and serve the chocolate babka at room temperature. Enjoy the rich, swirled layers of chocolate and sweet dough!

This chocolate babka is perfect for special occasions or as a sweet treat to share with family and friends. Feel free to customize the filling with cinnamon, nuts, or your favorite spreads for a delicious twist on this classic Jewish dessert!

Knishes (Stuffed Dough)

Ingredients:

For the Dough:

- 2 cups all-purpose flour
- 1/2 teaspoon salt
- 1/4 cup vegetable oil
- 1/2 cup water, plus more as needed

For the Potato Filling:

- 4 medium potatoes, peeled and diced
- 1 large onion, finely chopped
- 2 tablespoons vegetable oil
- Salt and pepper, to taste
- 1/2 teaspoon garlic powder (optional)
- 2 tablespoons chopped fresh parsley (optional)

Instructions:

Prepare the Dough:
- In a large mixing bowl, combine the flour and salt.
- Gradually add the vegetable oil and water, mixing until a dough forms.
- Knead the dough on a floured surface for about 5 minutes until smooth and elastic. Add more water if the dough is too dry or more flour if it's too sticky.
- Cover the dough with a damp towel and let it rest while you prepare the filling.

Make the Potato Filling:
- Boil the diced potatoes in a pot of salted water until tender, about 10-15 minutes. Drain and mash the potatoes with a potato masher or fork until smooth.
- In a skillet, heat vegetable oil over medium heat. Add the chopped onion and sauté until translucent and lightly golden.
- Add the sautéed onions to the mashed potatoes. Season with salt, pepper, garlic powder (if using), and chopped parsley (if using). Mix well to combine.

Assemble the Knishes:
- Preheat your oven to 375°F (190°C) and line a baking sheet with parchment paper.
- Divide the dough into 8 equal portions. Roll out each portion into a thin oval or rectangle shape on a floured surface.

Fill and Fold the Knishes:
- Spoon a portion of the potato filling onto one half of each dough piece, leaving a border around the edges.
- Fold the other half of the dough over the filling to enclose it, pressing the edges firmly to seal.
- You can crimp the edges with a fork for a decorative finish.

Bake the Knishes:
- Place the filled knishes on the prepared baking sheet.
- Brush the tops of the knishes with a little vegetable oil or egg wash (1 beaten egg mixed with 1 tablespoon water).
- Bake in the preheated oven for 25-30 minutes, or until golden brown and crispy.

Serve and Enjoy:
- Let the knishes cool slightly before serving.
- Serve the potato knishes warm as an appetizer or snack, optionally with mustard or dipping sauce on the side.

These homemade potato knishes are deliciously comforting and perfect for sharing with family and friends during Jewish holiday gatherings or any occasion. Feel free to experiment with different fillings such as spinach and cheese or meat and onions to create your favorite knish variations!

Chopped Liver

Ingredients:

- 1 pound chicken livers, trimmed of any connective tissue
- 2 large onions, finely chopped
- 4 hard-boiled eggs, peeled
- 4 tablespoons schmaltz (rendered chicken fat) or vegetable oil
- Salt and pepper, to taste
- Optional garnishes: chopped fresh parsley, sliced green onions

Instructions:

Cook the Chicken Livers:
- Rinse the chicken livers under cold water and pat them dry with paper towels.
- In a skillet or frying pan, heat 2 tablespoons of schmaltz (or vegetable oil) over medium-high heat.
- Add the chopped onions to the pan and sauté until golden and caramelized, about 8-10 minutes.
- Push the onions to the side of the pan and add the chicken livers in a single layer. Cook for about 3-4 minutes per side until cooked through but still slightly pink in the center.
- Remove the cooked chicken livers and onions from the heat and let them cool slightly.

Prepare the Eggs:
- Hard-boil the eggs by placing them in a saucepan of cold water. Bring to a boil over medium-high heat, then reduce the heat and simmer for 10 minutes. Drain the eggs and rinse them under cold water. Peel and chop the hard-boiled eggs.

Chop the Livers and Onions:
- In a food processor, pulse the cooked chicken livers, onions, and hard-boiled eggs until finely chopped. Alternatively, you can chop them by hand with a sharp knife.

Season and Mix:
- Transfer the chopped liver mixture to a bowl.
- Add the remaining 2 tablespoons of schmaltz (or vegetable oil) to the bowl.

- Season with salt and pepper to taste. Mix well to combine all the ingredients evenly.

Serve and Garnish:
- Transfer the chopped liver to a serving dish.
- Garnish with chopped fresh parsley or sliced green onions, if desired.
- Serve the chopped liver at room temperature as a spread on crackers, bread, or matzo.

Enjoy this classic chopped liver as part of your Jewish holiday feast or as a delicious appetizer for any occasion. The combination of flavors from the chicken livers, onions, and hard-boiled eggs is simply irresistible! Adjust the seasoning and texture to your liking and share this delightful dish with family and friends.

Blintzes (Cheese or Fruit-filled Crepes)

Ingredients:

For the Blintz Crepes:

- 1 cup all-purpose flour
- 1 1/2 cups milk
- 2 large eggs
- 2 tablespoons melted butter, plus more for cooking
- Pinch of salt

For the Cheese Filling:

- 1 pound farmer's cheese or ricotta cheese
- 1/4 cup granulated sugar (adjust to taste)
- 1 large egg
- 1 teaspoon vanilla extract
- Zest of 1 lemon (optional)
- Butter or oil, for cooking

For Serving:

- Sour cream
- Fruit preserves or fresh berries (optional)
- Powdered sugar (for dusting)

Instructions:

Make the Blintz Crepes:
- In a blender or mixing bowl, combine the flour, milk, eggs, melted butter, and salt. Blend or whisk until smooth.
- Heat a non-stick skillet or crepe pan over medium heat. Brush the skillet with melted butter.
- Pour a small ladleful of batter into the skillet, swirling to coat the bottom evenly.
- Cook the crepe for about 1-2 minutes until the edges start to lift and the bottom is golden brown. Flip and cook for another 1-2 minutes on the other side.

- Repeat with the remaining batter, stacking the cooked crepes on a plate and covering with a clean kitchen towel to keep them warm.

Prepare the Cheese Filling:
- In a mixing bowl, combine the farmer's cheese or ricotta cheese, sugar, egg, vanilla extract, and lemon zest (if using). Mix until smooth and well combined.

Fill and Fold the Blintzes:
- Place a cooked crepe on a clean work surface with the smoother side down.
- Spoon about 2 tablespoons of the cheese filling in the center of the crepe.
- Fold the bottom edge of the crepe over the filling, then fold in the sides, and roll up tightly like a burrito.
- Repeat with the remaining crepes and filling.

Cook the Blintzes:
- Heat a skillet over medium heat and add butter or oil.
- Place the filled blintzes seam-side down in the skillet.
- Cook for about 2-3 minutes on each side until golden brown and heated through.

Serve and Enjoy:
- Serve the warm blintzes with a dollop of sour cream and a spoonful of fruit preserves or fresh berries, if desired.
- Dust with powdered sugar before serving, if you like.
- Enjoy these delicious cheese blintzes as a sweet treat or special breakfast!

Feel free to customize your blintzes with different fillings like fruit preserves or berries for a sweet variation, or experiment with savory fillings for a delicious main course. Blintzes are versatile and can be enjoyed on their own or as part of a festive meal.

Stuffed Cabbage Rolls

Ingredients:

For the Cabbage Rolls:

- 1 large head of cabbage
- 1 pound ground beef (or a mixture of beef and pork)
- 1 cup cooked white rice
- 1 onion, finely chopped
- 2 cloves garlic, minced
- 1 egg, beaten
- 1/4 cup chopped fresh parsley
- Salt and pepper, to taste
- 1/2 teaspoon paprika
- 1/2 teaspoon dried thyme (optional)
- 1/4 teaspoon ground cinnamon (optional)

For the Tomato Sauce:

- 1 can (28 ounces) crushed tomatoes
- 1 can (14 ounces) tomato sauce
- 1/4 cup brown sugar
- 2 tablespoons lemon juice
- Salt and pepper, to taste

Instructions:

Prepare the Cabbage Leaves:
- Bring a large pot of salted water to a boil.
- Carefully remove the core from the cabbage and place the whole head of cabbage in the boiling water.
- Cook for about 5-7 minutes, then use tongs to remove the outer leaves that are soft and pliable. Continue cooking and removing leaves until you have about 12-14 large leaves.
- Trim the thick center rib from each cabbage leaf to make them easier to roll.

Make the Filling:
- In a large mixing bowl, combine the ground beef, cooked rice, chopped onion, minced garlic, beaten egg, chopped parsley, salt, pepper, paprika, thyme, and cinnamon (if using). Mix well to combine all ingredients.

Assemble the Cabbage Rolls:
- Place a cabbage leaf on a clean work surface.
- Spoon a portion of the filling (about 1/4 cup) onto the center of the leaf.
- Fold the sides of the leaf over the filling, then roll up from the bottom to enclose the filling, forming a tight roll.
- Repeat with the remaining cabbage leaves and filling.

Prepare the Tomato Sauce:
- In a large pot or Dutch oven, combine the crushed tomatoes, tomato sauce, brown sugar, lemon juice, salt, and pepper.
- Stir well to combine and bring the sauce to a simmer over medium heat.

Cook the Cabbage Rolls:
- Place the cabbage rolls seam-side down into the pot with the tomato sauce.
- Spoon some of the sauce over the tops of the cabbage rolls.
- Cover the pot with a lid and simmer over low heat for 1.5 to 2 hours, or until the cabbage rolls are tender and cooked through, and the flavors have melded together.

Serve and Enjoy:
- Carefully remove the cabbage rolls from the pot using tongs or a slotted spoon.
- Serve the stuffed cabbage rolls hot, spooning some of the tomato sauce over each roll.
- Enjoy these delicious and comforting stuffed cabbage rolls as a main course for a special meal!

Stuffed cabbage rolls are perfect for serving during Jewish holidays or any occasion when you're craving a hearty and satisfying dish. They can be made ahead of time and are even better the next day as the flavors continue to develop. Enjoy!

Kreplach (Meat Dumplings)

Ingredients:

For the Dough:

- 2 cups all-purpose flour
- 2 large eggs
- 1/2 teaspoon salt
- Water, as needed

For the Meat Filling:

- 1/2 pound ground beef or chicken
- 1 small onion, finely chopped
- 1 clove garlic, minced
- 1 tablespoon vegetable oil
- Salt and pepper, to taste
- 1/2 teaspoon paprika
- 1/2 teaspoon dried thyme or parsley
- Optional: 1-2 tablespoons chopped fresh parsley or dill

For Cooking and Serving:

- Chicken or beef broth, for boiling
- Chopped fresh parsley or dill, for garnish
- Sour cream or horseradish, for serving (optional)

Instructions:

Make the Dough:
- In a large mixing bowl, combine the flour, eggs, and salt.
- Gradually add water, a little at a time, mixing until the dough comes together and forms a ball.
- Knead the dough on a lightly floured surface for about 5 minutes until smooth and elastic. Cover with a damp towel and let it rest while you prepare the filling.

Prepare the Meat Filling:
- In a skillet, heat the vegetable oil over medium heat.

- Add the chopped onion and sauté until softened and translucent, about 3-4 minutes.
- Add the minced garlic and cook for another 1 minute until fragrant.
- Add the ground beef or chicken to the skillet, breaking it up with a spoon.
- Cook until the meat is browned and cooked through.
- Season with salt, pepper, paprika, dried thyme or parsley, and optional chopped fresh herbs.
- Remove from heat and let the filling cool slightly.

Assemble the Kreplach:

- Roll out the dough on a lightly floured surface into a thin sheet, about 1/8 inch thick.
- Use a round cookie cutter or drinking glass to cut out circles of dough, about 3 inches in diameter.
- Place a small spoonful of the meat filling in the center of each dough circle.
- Fold the dough over the filling to form a half-moon shape, pressing the edges together firmly to seal.
- You can crimp the edges with a fork for a decorative finish.

Cook the Kreplach:

- Bring a large pot of salted water or broth to a boil.
- Carefully drop the kreplach into the boiling water and cook for about 5-7 minutes, or until they float to the surface and are cooked through.
- Remove the cooked kreplach with a slotted spoon and drain well.

Serve the Kreplach:

- Serve the kreplach hot in chicken or beef broth, garnished with chopped fresh parsley or dill.
- Optionally, serve with a dollop of sour cream or horseradish on the side.

Enjoy these flavorful and comforting kreplach as a special treat during Jewish holidays or any time you crave a delicious dumpling dish! They can also be frozen before cooking for later enjoyment.

Chicken Schnitzel

Ingredients:

- 4 boneless, skinless chicken breasts
- Salt and pepper, to taste
- 1 cup all-purpose flour
- 2 large eggs, beaten
- 1 cup breadcrumbs (plain or seasoned)
- 1/2 cup grated Parmesan cheese (optional, for extra flavor)
- Vegetable oil, for frying
- Lemon wedges, for serving

Instructions:

Prepare the Chicken:
- Place each chicken breast between two sheets of plastic wrap or wax paper.
- Use a meat mallet or rolling pin to pound the chicken breasts to an even thickness of about 1/4 to 1/2 inch.
- Season the chicken breasts with salt and pepper on both sides.

Set Up Breading Station:
- Prepare three shallow bowls or plates:
    - Bowl 1: Place the flour and season with a bit of salt and pepper.
    - Bowl 2: Beat the eggs until well combined.
    - Bowl 3: Combine the breadcrumbs with grated Parmesan cheese (if using).

Bread the Chicken:
- Dredge each chicken breast in the flour, shaking off any excess.
- Dip the floured chicken breast into the beaten eggs, coating both sides.
- Press the chicken breast into the breadcrumb mixture, ensuring an even coating of breadcrumbs on both sides. Press gently to adhere the breadcrumbs.

Fry the Schnitzel:
- In a large skillet, heat about 1/4 inch of vegetable oil over medium-high heat.
- Carefully place the breaded chicken breasts into the hot oil, cooking in batches if needed to avoid overcrowding the pan.

- Fry the chicken schnitzel for about 3-4 minutes on each side, or until golden brown and cooked through. The internal temperature should reach 165°F (75°C).
- Transfer the cooked schnitzel to a plate lined with paper towels to drain excess oil.

Serve the Chicken Schnitzel:

- Serve the chicken schnitzel hot, garnished with lemon wedges on the side.
- Enjoy the crispy and flavorful chicken schnitzel as a main dish, alongside mashed potatoes, salad, or your favorite side dishes.

Chicken schnitzel is a versatile dish that can be enjoyed for weeknight dinners or served on special occasions. It's simple to prepare and loved by both kids and adults alike. Feel free to customize the seasoning of the breadcrumbs or add herbs like parsley or thyme for extra flavor. Enjoy your homemade chicken schnitzel!

Hamentashen (Filled Cookies)

Ingredients:

For the Cookie Dough:

- 2/3 cup unsalted butter, softened
- 3/4 cup granulated sugar
- 2 large eggs
- 1 teaspoon vanilla extract
- 3 cups all-purpose flour
- 1 1/2 teaspoons baking powder
- 1/4 teaspoon salt

For the Filling:

- Your choice of fruit preserves (such as apricot, raspberry, cherry)
- Poppy seed filling
- Chocolate spread
- Nutella
- Other sweet fillings of your choice

Instructions:

Prepare the Cookie Dough:
- In a large mixing bowl, cream together the softened butter and sugar until light and fluffy.
- Add the eggs and vanilla extract, and mix until well combined.
- In a separate bowl, whisk together the flour, baking powder, and salt.
- Gradually add the dry ingredients to the wet ingredients, mixing until a dough forms. If the dough is too sticky, you can refrigerate it for 30 minutes to firm up.

Roll Out the Dough:
- Preheat your oven to 375°F (190°C) and line baking sheets with parchment paper.
- On a lightly floured surface, roll out the dough to about 1/8 inch thickness.
- Use a round cookie cutter (about 3 inches in diameter) to cut out circles from the dough.

Fill and Shape the Hamentashen:

- Place a teaspoon of filling in the center of each dough circle.
- To shape the hamentashen, fold the sides of the circle up to create a triangle shape, pinching the corners together to seal the edges and leaving a small opening in the center to reveal the filling.

Bake the Hamentashen:
- Place the filled hamentashen on the prepared baking sheets.
- Bake in the preheated oven for 10-12 minutes, or until the edges are lightly golden.
- Remove from the oven and let the hamentashen cool on the baking sheets for a few minutes before transferring to a wire rack to cool completely.

Serve and Enjoy:
- Once cooled, serve the hamentashen and enjoy these delicious cookies filled with sweet goodness!
- Store any leftover hamentashen in an airtight container at room temperature for up to several days.

Feel free to get creative with the fillings and experiment with different flavors and combinations. Hamentashen are a festive treat perfect for celebrating Purim or enjoying as a delightful cookie any time of the year. Enjoy making and sharing these tasty hamentashen cookies with family and friends!

Sephardic Fish Stew

Ingredients:

- 1.5 pounds firm white fish fillets (such as cod, halibut, or tilapia), cut into large chunks
- 2 tablespoons olive oil
- 1 onion, finely chopped
- 4 cloves garlic, minced
- 1 red bell pepper, thinly sliced
- 1 yellow bell pepper, thinly sliced
- 1 can (14 ounces) diced tomatoes
- 2 tablespoons tomato paste
- 1 teaspoon paprika
- 1 teaspoon ground cumin
- 1/2 teaspoon ground coriander
- 1/2 teaspoon ground turmeric
- 1/4 teaspoon cayenne pepper (adjust to taste)
- Salt and pepper, to taste
- 1/2 cup water or fish stock
- Fresh cilantro or parsley, chopped (for garnish)
- Lemon wedges, for serving
- Cooked couscous or crusty bread, for serving

Instructions:

Prepare the Fish and Vegetables:
- Pat the fish fillets dry with paper towels and season with salt and pepper. Set aside.
- In a large skillet or Dutch oven, heat the olive oil over medium heat.
- Add the chopped onion and sauté until softened and translucent, about 5 minutes.
- Add the minced garlic and sliced bell peppers to the skillet. Cook for another 3-4 minutes until the peppers start to soften.

Make the Spice Mixture:
- Stir in the diced tomatoes and tomato paste into the skillet.

- Add the paprika, ground cumin, ground coriander, ground turmeric, cayenne pepper, salt, and pepper. Mix well to combine all the spices with the vegetables.

Simmer the Stew:
- Pour in the water or fish stock and bring the mixture to a simmer.
- Reduce the heat to low and let the stew simmer gently for about 10-15 minutes, allowing the flavors to meld together and the sauce to thicken slightly.

Add the Fish:
- Carefully place the fish fillets into the simmering sauce, nestling them into the vegetables.
- Cover the skillet or pot and continue to simmer for another 8-10 minutes, or until the fish is cooked through and flakes easily with a fork.

Serve the Sephardic Fish Stew:
- Taste and adjust seasoning with salt and pepper if needed.
- Sprinkle chopped fresh cilantro or parsley over the stew.
- Serve the Sephardic fish stew hot, accompanied by cooked couscous or crusty bread and lemon wedges on the side.

Enjoy this flavorful and aromatic Sephardic Fish Stew as a satisfying main course that's perfect for sharing with family and friends. The combination of spices and tender fish makes this dish a true delight!

Moroccan Carrot Salad

Ingredients:

- 1 pound carrots, peeled and grated or thinly sliced
- 2 tablespoons olive oil
- 1 clove garlic, minced
- 1 teaspoon ground cumin
- 1/2 teaspoon paprika
- 1/2 teaspoon ground cinnamon
- Salt and pepper, to taste
- Juice of 1 lemon
- 2 tablespoons chopped fresh cilantro or parsley
- 2 tablespoons chopped fresh mint (optional)
- 2 tablespoons golden raisins or currants (optional)
- 2 tablespoons chopped almonds or walnuts, toasted (optional)

Instructions:

Prepare the Carrots:
- Peel the carrots and grate them using a box grater or slice them thinly into matchsticks.

Cook the Carrots:
- In a large skillet or pot, heat the olive oil over medium heat.
- Add the minced garlic, ground cumin, paprika, and ground cinnamon to the skillet. Cook for about 1 minute until fragrant.
- Add the grated or sliced carrots to the skillet. Season with salt and pepper to taste.
- Stir to coat the carrots evenly with the spices and oil.
- Reduce the heat to low, cover the skillet, and cook the carrots for 8-10 minutes, stirring occasionally, until they are tender but still have a slight crunch.

Assemble the Salad:
- Transfer the cooked carrots to a serving bowl.
- Drizzle the lemon juice over the carrots and toss to combine.
- Let the carrots cool to room temperature.

Add Fresh Herbs and Toppings:

- Once the carrots have cooled, add the chopped fresh cilantro or parsley, and chopped fresh mint (if using).
- If desired, add golden raisins or currants for a touch of sweetness.
- Sprinkle toasted chopped almonds or walnuts over the salad for added texture and flavor.

Serve the Moroccan Carrot Salad:
- Toss the salad gently to combine all the ingredients.
- Taste and adjust seasoning with additional salt, pepper, or lemon juice if needed.
- Serve the Moroccan carrot salad at room temperature as a side dish or appetizer.

This Moroccan carrot salad is bursting with flavor and makes a wonderful addition to any meal. It can be served alongside grilled meats, couscous dishes, or as part of a mezze spread. Enjoy the sweet and savory flavors of this colorful salad inspired by Moroccan cuisine!

Israeli Couscous Salad

Ingredients:

- For the Salad:
    - 1 cup Israeli couscous
    - 1 cucumber, diced
    - 1 bell pepper (red, yellow, or orange), diced
    - 1 pint cherry tomatoes, halved
    - 1/2 red onion, finely chopped
    - 1/4 cup chopped fresh parsley
    - 1/4 cup chopped fresh mint
    - Optional additions: diced avocado, crumbled feta cheese, chopped olives
- For the Dressing:
    - 1/4 cup olive oil
    - 2 tablespoons fresh lemon juice
    - 1 tablespoon red wine vinegar
    - 1 garlic clove, minced
    - 1 teaspoon Dijon mustard
    - Salt and pepper, to taste

Instructions:

Cook the Israeli Couscous:
- In a pot of boiling salted water, cook the Israeli couscous according to package instructions until al dente, about 8-10 minutes. Drain and rinse under cold water to stop the cooking process. Set aside to cool.

Prepare the Vegetables and Herbs:
- Dice the cucumber, bell pepper, and red onion. Halve the cherry tomatoes. Chop the parsley and mint. Combine all in a large salad bowl.

Make the Dressing:
- In a small bowl, whisk together the olive oil, lemon juice, red wine vinegar, minced garlic, Dijon mustard, salt, and pepper until well combined.

Assemble the Salad:
- Add the cooled Israeli couscous to the bowl of vegetables and herbs.
- Pour the dressing over the salad and toss gently until everything is well coated.

Serve:
- Taste and adjust seasoning with more salt, pepper, or lemon juice if needed.

- If desired, add optional ingredients like diced avocado, crumbled feta cheese, or chopped olives.
- Serve chilled or at room temperature.

Tips and Variations:

- Add Protein: For a heartier salad, add cooked chickpeas, grilled chicken, shrimp, or tofu.
- Customize Vegetables: Feel free to use other fresh vegetables like diced zucchini, corn kernels, or roasted eggplant.
- Herb Substitutions: If you don't have parsley or mint, try using cilantro, basil, or dill.
- Make-Ahead: This salad can be made ahead of time and stored in the refrigerator. The flavors will meld together nicely.

Enjoy your Israeli couscous salad as a side dish or a light main course. It's perfect for picnics, potlucks, or as a refreshing summer meal.

Pomegranate Chicken

Ingredients:

- 4 boneless, skinless chicken breasts or thighs
- Salt and pepper, to taste
- 2 tablespoons olive oil
- 1 onion, finely chopped
- 3 cloves garlic, minced
- 1 cup chicken broth
- 1/2 cup pomegranate juice
- 1/4 cup honey or maple syrup
- 2 tablespoons balsamic vinegar
- 1/2 cup pomegranate arils (seeds), plus extra for garnish
- Fresh parsley or cilantro, chopped (for garnish)

Instructions:

Season and Sear the Chicken:
- Season the chicken breasts or thighs with salt and pepper.
- In a large skillet or pan, heat olive oil over medium-high heat.
- Add the chicken to the skillet and cook until browned on both sides, about 3-4 minutes per side. Remove the chicken from the skillet and set aside.

Prepare the Sauce:
- In the same skillet, add chopped onion and garlic. Cook until softened and translucent, about 2-3 minutes.

Simmer the Chicken:
- Pour in chicken broth, pomegranate juice, honey or maple syrup, and balsamic vinegar. Stir to combine.
- Return the chicken to the skillet, turning to coat it in the sauce.
- Bring the mixture to a simmer, then reduce heat to low. Cover and let it cook for 15-20 minutes, or until the chicken is cooked through and tender.

Add Pomegranate Arils:
- Stir in the pomegranate arils (seeds) during the last 5 minutes of cooking, allowing them to infuse into the sauce.

Serve:
- Transfer the chicken to a serving platter or individual plates.
- Spoon the sauce and pomegranate arils over the chicken.
- Garnish with additional pomegranate arils and chopped fresh parsley or cilantro.

Tips and Variations:

- Pomegranate Molasses: If you don't have pomegranate juice, you can use pomegranate molasses diluted with water for a similar flavor.
- Additional Flavors: Feel free to add a pinch of cinnamon or cumin to the sauce for extra depth of flavor.
- Side Dish Suggestions: Serve the pomegranate chicken over couscous, rice, or quinoa, alongside roasted vegetables or a fresh green salad.

This Pomegranate Chicken dish is both visually stunning and delicious, making it a wonderful centerpiece for any festive meal. The sweet and tangy flavors of the pomegranate complement the tender chicken perfectly, creating a dish that's sure to impress your guests during Jewish holiday celebrations.

Lamb Tagine

Ingredients:

- 2 lbs lamb shoulder or leg, cut into chunks
- 2 tablespoons olive oil
- 1 large onion, finely chopped
- 3 cloves garlic, minced
- 1 tablespoon grated fresh ginger
- 2 teaspoons ground cumin
- 2 teaspoons ground coriander
- 1 teaspoon ground cinnamon
- 1/2 teaspoon ground turmeric
- 1/2 teaspoon ground paprika
- Pinch of saffron threads (optional)
- Salt and pepper, to taste
- 1/2 cup dried apricots, halved
- 1/2 cup pitted green olives
- 1 preserved lemon, pulp discarded, rind thinly sliced
- 1 tablespoon honey
- 2 cups chicken or lamb broth
- Chopped fresh cilantro or parsley, for garnish
- Cooked couscous or rice, for serving

Instructions:

Prepare the Lamb:
- In a large tagine or heavy-bottomed pot, heat olive oil over medium-high heat.
- Season the lamb chunks with salt and pepper, then add them to the pot in batches to brown on all sides. Remove the browned lamb and set aside.

Saute the Aromatics:
- In the same pot, add chopped onion and sauté until softened and translucent, about 5 minutes.
- Stir in minced garlic, grated ginger, ground cumin, ground coriander, ground cinnamon, turmeric, paprika, and saffron threads (if using). Cook for another 1-2 minutes until fragrant.

Combine and Simmer:
- Return the browned lamb to the pot, along with dried apricots, green olives, preserved lemon slices, and honey.
- Pour in chicken or lamb broth, enough to cover the lamb. Bring the mixture to a simmer.

Cook the Tagine:
- Reduce the heat to low, cover the pot (or use a tagine lid if using), and let the tagine simmer gently for 2-3 hours, or until the lamb is tender and the flavors have melded together. Stir occasionally and add more broth if needed to keep it moist.

Serve:
- Taste and adjust seasoning with salt and pepper if needed.
- Garnish the lamb tagine with chopped fresh cilantro or parsley before serving.
- Serve the lamb tagine hot over cooked couscous or rice.

Tips and Variations:

- Substitute Ingredients: Feel free to substitute dried apricots with other dried fruits like raisins or prunes.
- Preserved Lemon: If you don't have preserved lemon, you can use fresh lemon zest for a similar citrusy flavor.
- Spice Level: Adjust the amount of spices according to your taste preferences. Add a pinch of cayenne pepper for extra heat if desired.
- Make-Ahead: Lamb tagine tastes even better the next day after the flavors have had time to develop, so it's a great dish to prepare in advance.

Enjoy this aromatic and flavorful lamb tagine as part of your holiday feast or any special gathering. The tender lamb, combined with the sweetness of dried fruits and the tanginess of olives and preserved lemon, creates a truly delightful dish that will impress your guests.

Spinach Borekas

Ingredients:

For the Filling:

- 1 tablespoon olive oil
- 1 onion, finely chopped
- 2 garlic cloves, minced
- 1 pound fresh spinach, washed and chopped
- Salt and pepper, to taste
- 1/4 teaspoon nutmeg (optional)
- 1/2 cup crumbled feta cheese (optional)

For the Pastry Dough:

- 1 package (about 17.3 oz) frozen puff pastry sheets, thawed (or use homemade dough)
- 1 egg, beaten (for egg wash)
- Sesame seeds or poppy seeds (for sprinkling, optional)

Instructions:

Prepare the Spinach Filling:
- Heat olive oil in a large skillet over medium heat.
- Add chopped onion and sauté until softened and translucent, about 3-4 minutes.
- Add minced garlic and cook for another 1 minute.
- Add chopped spinach to the skillet and cook until wilted, stirring frequently.
- Season with salt, pepper, and nutmeg (if using).
- Remove from heat and let the spinach mixture cool slightly. Stir in crumbled feta cheese (if using).

Assemble the Borekas:
- Preheat your oven to 375°F (190°C) and line a baking sheet with parchment paper.
- Roll out the thawed puff pastry sheets on a lightly floured surface. Cut each sheet into squares or rectangles, about 4-5 inches in size.

Fill and Fold the Borekas:
- Place a spoonful of the spinach filling onto one half of each pastry square.
- Fold the other half of the pastry over the filling to create a triangle or rectangle shape.

- Use a fork to press and seal the edges of the borekas.

Bake the Borekas:
- Place the filled borekas on the prepared baking sheet.
- Brush the tops of the borekas with beaten egg (egg wash) to give them a golden color when baked.
- Sprinkle sesame seeds or poppy seeds on top (optional).
- Bake in the preheated oven for 15-20 minutes, or until the borekas are puffed up and golden brown.

Serve:
- Remove the spinach borekas from the oven and let them cool slightly before serving.
- Enjoy warm as a delightful appetizer or side dish.

Tips and Variations:

- Variations: You can substitute the spinach with other fillings such as cheese, mushrooms, or mashed potatoes.
- Make-Ahead: You can assemble the spinach borekas in advance and refrigerate or freeze them before baking. Simply bake them straight from the refrigerator or freezer, adjusting the baking time accordingly.
- Serve with Dips: Serve the spinach borekas with a side of tahini sauce, yogurt sauce, or your favorite dipping sauce.

These homemade spinach borekas are sure to be a hit at any gathering or holiday celebration. They're crispy on the outside, packed with savory spinach and cheese on the inside, making them a delightful treat for everyone to enjoy.

Shakshuka

Ingredients:

- 2 tablespoons olive oil
- 1 onion, finely chopped
- 1 red bell pepper, seeded and diced
- 3 cloves garlic, minced
- 1 teaspoon ground cumin
- 1 teaspoon paprika
- 1/2 teaspoon chili powder (adjust to taste)
- 1 can (28 oz) diced tomatoes, with juices
- Salt and pepper, to taste
- 4-6 eggs (depending on the size of your skillet)
- Fresh parsley or cilantro, chopped (for garnish)
- Crumbled feta cheese or goat cheese (optional, for serving)
- Crusty bread or pita, for serving

Instructions:

Saute the Vegetables:
- Heat olive oil in a large skillet or cast-iron pan over medium heat.
- Add chopped onion and diced bell pepper. Cook until softened, about 5-7 minutes.
- Add minced garlic, ground cumin, paprika, and chili powder. Stir and cook for another 1-2 minutes until fragrant.

Make the Tomato Sauce:
- Pour in the diced tomatoes with their juices. Season with salt and pepper.
- Bring the mixture to a simmer and cook for about 10-15 minutes, stirring occasionally, until the sauce has thickened slightly.

Poach the Eggs:
- Using a spoon, create small wells or indentations in the tomato sauce.
- Crack each egg directly into a well in the sauce, spacing them evenly.
- Season the eggs with a bit of salt and pepper.

Simmer and Cook the Eggs:
- Cover the skillet with a lid and reduce the heat to medium-low.
- Let the shakshuka simmer gently for about 8-10 minutes, or until the egg whites are set but the yolks are still runny (cook longer if you prefer firmer yolks).

Serve:

- Remove the skillet from heat.
- Sprinkle chopped fresh parsley or cilantro over the shakshuka.
- If desired, crumble feta cheese or goat cheese over the top.
- Serve the shakshuka directly from the skillet, with crusty bread or pita on the side for dipping and scooping up the delicious sauce.

Tips and Variations:

- Spice Level: Adjust the amount of chili powder based on your spice preference.
- Additional Ingredients: Feel free to add other ingredients like cooked chickpeas, spinach, or crumbled sausage to the sauce.
- Make-Ahead: You can prepare the tomato sauce ahead of time and poach the eggs just before serving.
- Dietary Preferences: Shakshuka is naturally gluten-free and can be made vegetarian by omitting the cheese or adding more vegetables.

Enjoy this hearty and comforting shakshuka with its rich tomato sauce and perfectly poached eggs. It's a versatile dish that's satisfying and full of flavor, making it a great addition to any holiday or special meal.

Halva (Sesame Sweet)

Ingredients:

- 1 cup tahini (sesame paste)
- 1 cup granulated sugar
- 1/2 cup water
- 1 teaspoon vanilla extract
- Pinch of salt
- Optional add-ins: chopped nuts (like pistachios or almonds), chocolate chips, dried fruit (such as raisins)

Instructions:

Prepare the Syrup:
- In a small saucepan, combine the sugar and water over medium heat.
- Stir until the sugar dissolves completely, and the mixture comes to a gentle boil.

Cook the Syrup:
- Reduce the heat to low and let the syrup simmer for about 5-7 minutes, without stirring, until it reaches a slightly thickened consistency (about 225°F or 110°C on a candy thermometer).
- Remove the syrup from heat and set aside to cool slightly.

Mix the Tahini:
- While the syrup is cooling, place the tahini in a mixing bowl.
- Gradually pour the warm syrup into the tahini, stirring continuously until well combined and smooth.

Add Flavorings:
- Stir in the vanilla extract and a pinch of salt. Mix until incorporated.

Optional Add-Ins:
- If desired, fold in chopped nuts, chocolate chips, or dried fruit into the halva mixture for added texture and flavor.

Shape and Serve:
- Line a small baking dish or mold with parchment paper.
- Transfer the halva mixture into the lined dish, spreading it evenly with a spatula.

Chill and Set:
- Place the halva in the refrigerator to cool and set for at least 2 hours, or until firm.

Slice and Enjoy:

- Once set, remove the halva from the refrigerator and slice it into pieces.
- Serve the sesame halva at room temperature as a sweet treat or dessert.

Tips and Variations:

- Texture Adjustments: For a softer halva, use less tahini or more syrup. For a firmer halva, increase the tahini ratio.
- Flavor Variations: Experiment with different flavorings such as rose water, orange blossom water, or cinnamon for unique variations.
- Storage: Store leftover halva in an airtight container in the refrigerator for up to one week. Bring it to room temperature before serving.

This homemade sesame halva is a wonderful way to enjoy a classic sweet treat that's both simple and delicious. Whether you serve it during a holiday celebration or as a special dessert, this sesame halva is sure to be a hit with its nutty, sweet flavors and melt-in-your-mouth texture.

Falafel with Tahini Sauce

Ingredients:

For the Falafel:

- 1 cup dried chickpeas (or use canned chickpeas, drained and rinsed)
- 1 small onion, roughly chopped
- 3 cloves garlic, minced
- 1/2 cup fresh parsley, chopped
- 1/2 cup fresh cilantro, chopped
- 1 teaspoon ground cumin
- 1 teaspoon ground coriander
- 1/2 teaspoon baking soda
- Salt and pepper, to taste
- Vegetable oil, for frying

For the Tahini Sauce:

- 1/2 cup tahini (sesame paste)
- 1/4 cup water (or more for desired consistency)
- 2 tablespoons fresh lemon juice
- 1 clove garlic, minced
- Salt, to taste

For Serving:

- Pita bread or wraps
- Lettuce, tomato, cucumber (for garnish)
- Pickles or pickled vegetables

Instructions:

Prepare the Falafel Mixture:
- If using dried chickpeas, soak them in water overnight. Drain well before using.
- In a food processor, combine chickpeas, chopped onion, minced garlic, parsley, cilantro, ground cumin, ground coriander, baking soda, salt, and pepper.
- Pulse the mixture until it forms a coarse paste. You may need to scrape down the sides of the food processor bowl a few times to ensure even blending.

Shape the Falafel:
- Transfer the falafel mixture to a bowl. Using your hands, shape the mixture into small patties or balls, about 1.5 inches in diameter.

Fry the Falafel:
- In a large skillet or deep fryer, heat vegetable oil over medium heat.
- Carefully add the falafel patties to the hot oil, a few at a time, without overcrowding the pan.
- Fry the falafel for 3-4 minutes per side, or until golden brown and crispy. Use a slotted spoon to remove them from the oil and transfer to a paper towel-lined plate to drain excess oil.

Make the Tahini Sauce:
- In a small bowl, whisk together tahini, water, fresh lemon juice, minced garlic, and salt until smooth and creamy. Add more water if needed to achieve your desired consistency.

Assemble and Serve:
- Warm the pita bread or wraps.
- Stuff the pita with falafel, lettuce, tomato, cucumber, and pickles.
- Drizzle tahini sauce over the falafel or serve it on the side for dipping.
- Serve falafel wraps immediately and enjoy!

Tips and Variations:

- Baking Option: If you prefer a healthier alternative, you can bake the falafel patties in a preheated oven at 375°F (190°C) for 25-30 minutes, flipping halfway through.
- Herb Variations: Feel free to adjust the amount of fresh herbs (parsley and cilantro) based on your preference.
- Spice Level: Add a pinch of cayenne pepper or chili flakes to the falafel mixture for a spicier kick.
- Make-Ahead: You can prepare the falafel mixture in advance and refrigerate it until ready to fry or bake.

Enjoy this delicious homemade falafel with tahini sauce as a satisfying meal or appetizer during your holiday gatherings or any occasion. The combination of crispy falafel, fresh vegetables, and creamy tahini sauce wrapped in warm pita bread is simply irresistible!

Jerusalem Bagels

Ingredients:

- 4 cups all-purpose flour
- 2 teaspoons instant yeast
- 2 teaspoons sugar
- 1 1/2 teaspoons salt
- 1 1/2 cups warm water
- 2 tablespoons sesame seeds (optional, for topping)
- Olive oil or melted butter, for brushing

Instructions:

Mix the Dough:
- In a large mixing bowl, combine the flour, instant yeast, sugar, and salt.
- Gradually add the warm water to the dry ingredients, mixing until a dough forms.
- Knead the dough on a floured surface for about 8-10 minutes until it becomes smooth and elastic.

Let the Dough Rise:
- Place the dough in a lightly oiled bowl, cover with a clean kitchen towel, and let it rise in a warm place for about 1-1.5 hours, or until doubled in size.

Shape the Bagels:
- After the dough has risen, punch it down and divide it into 8 equal portions.
- Roll each portion into a rope about 10 inches long.
- Shape each rope into an oval or circle, overlapping the ends slightly and pinching them together to seal.

Preheat the Oven:
- Preheat your oven to 400°F (200°C) and line a baking sheet with parchment paper.

Final Rise and Topping:
- Place the shaped bagels on the prepared baking sheet, leaving space between them.
- Cover the bagels with a clean kitchen towel and let them rise for another 20-30 minutes.

Bake the Bagels:
- Brush the risen bagels with olive oil or melted butter.

- Sprinkle sesame seeds evenly over the tops of the bagels (if using).
- Bake in the preheated oven for 15-20 minutes, or until the bagels are golden brown and sound hollow when tapped on the bottom.

Cool and Serve:
- Allow the Jerusalem bagels to cool slightly on a wire rack before serving.
- Enjoy warm or at room temperature with your favorite spreads or dips, such as labneh, hummus, or za'atar.

Tips and Variations:

- Sesame-Free Option: If you prefer Jerusalem bagels without sesame seeds, you can omit the topping or use other toppings like poppy seeds, nigella seeds, or coarse salt.
- Sweet Variation: Add a touch more sugar to the dough for a slightly sweeter flavor, reminiscent of traditional Jerusalem bagels.
- Storage: Store leftover bagels in an airtight container at room temperature for 2-3 days, or freeze them for longer storage.

These homemade Jerusalem bagels are a wonderful addition to any meal or snack, and they're perfect for holiday gatherings or casual get-togethers. Enjoy their unique flavor and shape, and customize them with your favorite toppings for a delicious taste of Middle Eastern cuisine.

Sabich (Eggplant Sandwich)

Ingredients:

For the Sabich Sandwich:

- 1 large eggplant, cut into 1/2-inch slices
- Salt, for seasoning
- Vegetable oil, for frying
- 4 large eggs, hard-boiled and sliced
- 4 pita breads or flatbreads, warmed
- Israeli salad (see recipe below)
- Tahini sauce (store-bought or homemade, see recipe below)
- Amba (pickled mango condiment), optional
- Zhoug (spicy cilantro sauce), optional

For the Israeli Salad:

- 2 medium tomatoes, diced
- 1 cucumber, diced
- 1/2 red onion, finely chopped
- 1/4 cup chopped fresh parsley
- Juice of 1 lemon
- 2 tablespoons olive oil
- Salt and pepper, to taste

For the Tahini Sauce:

- 1/2 cup tahini (sesame paste)
- Juice of 1 lemon
- 1 garlic clove, minced
- 1/2 teaspoon salt
- Water, as needed to thin the sauce

Instructions:

Prepare the Israeli Salad:
- In a bowl, combine diced tomatoes, diced cucumber, chopped red onion, chopped parsley, lemon juice, olive oil, salt, and pepper. Toss well to combine. Set aside.

Make the Tahini Sauce:
- In another bowl, whisk together tahini, lemon juice, minced garlic, and salt.

- Gradually add water, a little at a time, and whisk until the sauce is smooth and creamy. Adjust the consistency to your liking by adding more water if needed. Set aside.

Fry the Eggplant:
- Sprinkle eggplant slices with salt and let them sit for about 15 minutes to release excess moisture.
- Pat the eggplant slices dry with paper towels.
- Heat vegetable oil in a skillet over medium-high heat.
- Fry the eggplant slices in batches until golden brown and tender, about 3-4 minutes per side. Transfer to a paper towel-lined plate to drain excess oil.

Assemble the Sabich Sandwich:
- Warm the pita breads or flatbreads.
- Open each pita and spread a generous amount of tahini sauce inside.
- Layer the fried eggplant slices, sliced hard-boiled eggs, Israeli salad, and any optional condiments (amba, zhoug) inside the pita.
- Fold or roll up the pita to enclose the filling.

Serve and Enjoy:
- Serve the Sabich sandwiches immediately while warm.
- Enjoy this delicious and flavorful Israeli eggplant sandwich with your favorite sides or additional condiments.

Tips and Variations:

- Condiments: Feel free to customize your Sabich sandwich with additional condiments such as pickles, hot sauce, or chopped herbs.
- Make-Ahead: Prepare the components (Israeli salad, tahini sauce, fried eggplant) in advance and assemble the sandwiches just before serving.
- Vegetarian Option: Omit the eggs for a vegetarian version of Sabich.

Enjoy making and savoring this authentic Israeli Sabich sandwich, packed with delicious flavors and textures. It's a delightful dish that's perfect for sharing with family and friends during Jewish holidays or any occasion!

Tahini Cookies

Ingredients:

- 1/2 cup unsalted butter, softened
- 3/4 cup granulated sugar
- 1/2 cup tahini (well-stirred)
- 1 large egg
- 1 teaspoon vanilla extract
- 1 1/2 cups all-purpose flour
- 1/2 teaspoon baking powder
- 1/4 teaspoon baking soda
- 1/4 teaspoon salt
- Optional toppings: sesame seeds, flaky sea salt, chopped nuts

Instructions:

Preheat the Oven:
- Preheat your oven to 350°F (175°C) and line a baking sheet with parchment paper.

Cream Butter and Sugar:
- In a mixing bowl, cream together softened butter and granulated sugar until light and fluffy.

Add Tahini and Wet Ingredients:
- Add tahini, egg, and vanilla extract to the butter-sugar mixture. Mix until well combined.

Combine Dry Ingredients:
- In a separate bowl, whisk together all-purpose flour, baking powder, baking soda, and salt.

Mix the Dough:
- Gradually add the dry ingredients to the wet ingredients, mixing until a soft cookie dough forms.

Shape and Bake the Cookies:
- Roll tablespoon-sized portions of dough into balls and place them on the prepared baking sheet, spacing them a few inches apart.
- Use a fork to gently flatten each cookie ball and create a crisscross pattern on top.

Add Toppings (Optional):
- Sprinkle sesame seeds, flaky sea salt, or chopped nuts on top of each cookie for added flavor and texture.

Bake:
- Bake the cookies in the preheated oven for 10-12 minutes, or until the edges are lightly golden.

Cool and Enjoy:
- Allow the cookies to cool on the baking sheet for a few minutes before transferring them to a wire rack to cool completely.

Tips and Variations:

- Tahini Variation: Use a good quality tahini that is well-stirred and creamy for the best flavor and texture.
- Texture: For a softer cookie, slightly underbake them and let them cool completely on the baking sheet.
- Storage: Store cooled tahini cookies in an airtight container at room temperature for up to one week.

These tahini cookies are perfect for serving as a sweet treat during Jewish holidays or any occasion. They pair wonderfully with a cup of tea or coffee, and their unique sesame flavor makes them stand out from traditional cookie recipes. Enjoy baking and indulging in these delightful tahini cookies!

Yemenite Soup

Ingredients:

- 1 pound (450g) beef stew meat, cut into small cubes
- 2 tablespoons vegetable oil
- 1 large onion, chopped
- 3 cloves garlic, minced
- 2 carrots, peeled and diced
- 2 celery stalks, diced
- 1 large potato, peeled and diced
- 1 bell pepper, diced (optional)
- 2 tomatoes, diced
- 2 tablespoons tomato paste
- 1 tablespoon hawaij spice mix (see recipe below)
- Salt and black pepper, to taste
- 8 cups (2 liters) beef or vegetable broth
- Fresh cilantro or parsley, chopped (for garnish)

For Hawaij Spice Mix:

- 1 tablespoon ground cumin
- 1 tablespoon ground turmeric
- 1 tablespoon ground coriander
- 1 tablespoon ground black pepper
- 1 teaspoon ground cardamom
- 1/2 teaspoon ground cloves

Instructions:

Prepare the Hawaij Spice Mix:
- In a small bowl, combine all the spices for the hawaij mix. Set aside.

Make the Soup:
- In a large pot or Dutch oven, heat the vegetable oil over medium-high heat. Add the chopped onions and sauté until they begin to soften.
- Add the minced garlic and continue to sauté for another minute.
- Add the beef cubes to the pot and brown them on all sides.
- Stir in the carrots, celery, potato, bell pepper (if using), and diced tomatoes. Cook for a few minutes until the vegetables start to soften.

- Add the tomato paste, hawaij spice mix, salt, and black pepper. Stir well to coat everything in the spices.
- Pour in the beef or vegetable broth and bring the soup to a boil.
- Reduce the heat to low, cover the pot, and simmer the soup for about 1 to 1.5 hours, or until the beef is tender and the vegetables are fully cooked.

Serve:
- Taste and adjust seasoning with more salt and pepper, if needed.
- Ladle the Yemenite Soup into bowls and garnish with freshly chopped cilantro or parsley.

Enjoy!
- Serve the soup hot with crusty bread or pita on the side. This hearty and flavorful Yemenite Soup is perfect for a comforting meal.

This recipe can be customized based on personal preferences. Some variations include adding chickpeas, lentils, or using different cuts of meat like lamb. Yemenite Soup is not only delicious but also a warming and satisfying dish that's great for sharing with family and friends.

Turkish Delight

Ingredients:

- 2 cups granulated sugar
- 1 ½ cups water
- 1 cup cornstarch
- 1 teaspoon cream of tartar
- 1 ½ tablespoons rosewater (or other flavoring like orange blossom water or lemon juice)
- Food coloring (optional)
- Powdered sugar, for coating

Instructions:

Prepare the Pan:
- Lightly grease an 8x8 inch (20x20 cm) baking dish with oil and line it with parchment paper. Dust the parchment paper with cornstarch to prevent sticking.

Make the Sugar Syrup:
- In a medium saucepan, combine the sugar and water over medium heat. Stir until the sugar dissolves completely.
- Add the cream of tartar to the sugar syrup and insert a candy thermometer into the mixture.

Cook the Syrup:
- Bring the sugar syrup to a boil and continue cooking without stirring until it reaches the soft-ball stage (240°F/115°C). This will take about 15-20 minutes.

Prepare the Cornstarch Mixture:
- While the syrup is cooking, mix the cornstarch with 1 cup of water in a separate bowl. Whisk until smooth.

Combine and Cook:
- Once the sugar syrup reaches the right temperature, slowly pour the cornstarch mixture into the syrup, stirring constantly to prevent lumps.
- Reduce the heat to low and continue stirring the mixture until it thickens and becomes a smooth, translucent paste. This will take about 15-20 minutes.

Add Flavoring and Color:
- Stir in the rosewater (or other flavoring of your choice) and food coloring (if using). Mix well until the flavor and color are evenly distributed.

Pour and Set:
- Immediately pour the hot mixture into the prepared baking dish. Smooth the top with a spatula or knife.

Cool and Cut:
- Allow the Turkish Delight to cool at room temperature for several hours or overnight until set and firm.

Coat and Serve:
- Once set, lift the Turkish Delight out of the pan using the parchment paper. Dust a cutting board with cornstarch and invert the Turkish Delight onto the board.
- Cut the Turkish Delight into small squares or rectangles using a sharp knife. Toss each piece in powdered sugar to prevent sticking.

Store:
- Store the Turkish Delight pieces in an airtight container, separating layers with parchment paper to prevent sticking. Enjoy this sweet treat as a delightful snack or dessert!

This homemade Turkish Delight is a wonderful treat to make for special occasions or to enjoy with family and friends. The flavor variations are endless, so feel free to experiment with different extracts and colors to create your favorite version of this classic confectionary.

Sufganiyot (Jelly Donuts)

Ingredients:

- 2 ¼ teaspoons (1 packet) active dry yeast
- ¼ cup warm water (about 110°F/43°C)
- 3 ½ cups all-purpose flour
- ¼ cup granulated sugar
- ½ teaspoon salt
- 1 teaspoon ground nutmeg
- 1 teaspoon vanilla extract
- 3 large eggs
- ¾ cup warm milk
- 3 tablespoons unsalted butter, softened
- Vegetable oil, for frying
- Raspberry jam or jelly, or other preferred filling
- Powdered sugar, for dusting

Instructions:

Activate the Yeast:
- In a small bowl, dissolve the yeast in the warm water. Let it sit for 5-10 minutes until foamy.

Prepare the Dough:
- In a large mixing bowl or the bowl of a stand mixer fitted with a dough hook, combine the flour, sugar, salt, and nutmeg.
- Add the activated yeast mixture, vanilla extract, eggs, warm milk, and softened butter to the dry ingredients.
- Mix on low speed until a soft dough forms. Increase the speed to medium and knead the dough for about 5-7 minutes until it's smooth and elastic. If kneading by hand, knead on a lightly floured surface.

First Rise:
- Place the dough in a greased bowl, cover with a clean kitchen towel or plastic wrap, and let it rise in a warm place for 1-2 hours, or until doubled in size.

Shape the Donuts:
- Once the dough has risen, punch it down gently to deflate. Roll out the dough on a lightly floured surface to about ¼-inch thickness.
- Using a round cookie cutter or drinking glass, cut out circles of dough about 2-3 inches in diameter. Place the dough circles on a parchment-lined

baking sheet, cover with a towel, and let them rise again for 30-45 minutes.

Fry the Donuts:
- In a deep, heavy-bottomed pot or deep fryer, heat vegetable oil to 350°F (175°C).
- Carefully add a few donuts to the hot oil, being careful not to overcrowd the pot. Fry for about 1-2 minutes on each side, or until golden brown and puffed.
- Remove the fried donuts with a slotted spoon and place them on a paper towel-lined plate to drain excess oil. Repeat with the remaining dough circles.

Fill the Donuts:
- Once the donuts have cooled slightly, use a piping bag fitted with a round tip to inject raspberry jam or preferred filling into each donut. You can also use a small knife to make a slit in the side of each donut and spoon in the filling.

Dust and Serve:
- Dust the filled sufganiyot generously with powdered sugar.

Enjoy:
- Serve the sufganiyot warm or at room temperature. They are best enjoyed fresh on the day they are made.

These homemade sufganiyot are a delightful treat for Hanukkah celebrations or any occasion. Feel free to get creative with different fillings such as chocolate, custard, or even savory options like cheese. Enjoy the festive sweetness of these jelly-filled donuts!

Lemon Garlic Hummus

Ingredients:

- 1 can (15 oz) chickpeas (garbanzo beans), drained and rinsed
- 3 tablespoons tahini (sesame seed paste)
- 2-3 tablespoons fresh lemon juice (adjust to taste)
- 2 garlic cloves, minced
- ½ teaspoon salt (adjust to taste)
- ¼ teaspoon ground cumin
- 3 tablespoons extra virgin olive oil
- 2-3 tablespoons water (adjust for desired consistency)
- Optional garnish: chopped fresh parsley, paprika, or additional olive oil

Instructions:

Prepare the Chickpeas:
- Drain and rinse the chickpeas thoroughly under cold water.

Blend Ingredients:
- In a food processor, combine the chickpeas, tahini, fresh lemon juice, minced garlic, salt, and ground cumin.
- Pulse the mixture until it starts to blend together.

Add Olive Oil:
- While the food processor is running, gradually drizzle in the extra virgin olive oil. Scrape down the sides of the bowl as needed.

Adjust Consistency:
- With the food processor running, slowly add water, 1 tablespoon at a time, until the hummus reaches your desired creamy consistency. Continue blending until smooth and creamy.

Taste and Adjust Seasoning:
- Taste the hummus and adjust the lemon juice, garlic, and salt to your preference. Add more lemon juice for a tangier flavor, more garlic for a stronger garlic taste, or more salt to enhance the flavors.

Serve:
- Transfer the Lemon Garlic Hummus to a serving bowl.

Garnish:
- Drizzle with a little extra virgin olive oil and sprinkle with chopped fresh parsley or a dash of paprika for color and flavor.

Enjoy:

- Serve the Lemon Garlic Hummus with pita bread, fresh vegetables (such as cucumber, carrots, or bell peppers), or use it as a spread on sandwiches and wraps.

Storage:
- Store leftover hummus in an airtight container in the refrigerator for up to 4-5 days. Before serving, let it come to room temperature or drizzle with a little olive oil and stir to refresh.

This Lemon Garlic Hummus is easy to make and bursting with flavor. Customize it by adjusting the lemon, garlic, or salt levels according to your taste preferences. It's a versatile and healthy dip or spread that's perfect for snacks, appetizers, or light meals. Enjoy!

Israeli Salad

Ingredients:

- 2 large tomatoes, diced
- 1 cucumber, diced
- 1 red bell pepper, diced
- 1 green bell pepper, diced
- 1 small red onion, finely chopped
- 1/4 cup chopped fresh parsley
- 1/4 cup chopped fresh mint (optional)
- Juice of 1-2 lemons
- 2-3 tablespoons extra virgin olive oil
- Salt and black pepper, to taste

Instructions:

Prepare the Vegetables:
- Wash and dice the tomatoes, cucumber, red bell pepper, and green bell pepper into small, bite-sized pieces. Place them in a large mixing bowl.

Chop the Onion and Herbs:
- Finely chop the red onion and add it to the bowl with the diced vegetables.
- Chop the fresh parsley and mint (if using) and add them to the bowl as well.

Dress the Salad:
- Drizzle the lemon juice and extra virgin olive oil over the vegetables.

Season:
- Season the salad with salt and black pepper, to taste.

Toss Well:
- Gently toss all the ingredients together until everything is well combined and coated with the dressing.

Chill (Optional):
- For best flavor, let the Israeli Salad chill in the refrigerator for about 30 minutes to allow the flavors to meld together.

Serve:
- Transfer the Israeli Salad to a serving dish or individual plates.

Enjoy:
- Israeli Salad is best served fresh as a side dish or topping. It pairs well with grilled meats, falafel, pita bread, or as part of a mezze platter.

Tips for Variations:

- Additions: Feel free to add other vegetables such as radishes, celery, or chopped lettuce for extra crunch and flavor.
- Spices: For extra flavor, consider adding a sprinkle of sumac or za'atar seasoning to the salad.
- Customize: Adjust the lemon juice and olive oil quantities according to your taste preference. Some like it more tangy, while others prefer it more mellow.

Israeli Salad is a simple yet vibrant dish that showcases the freshness of Mediterranean ingredients. It's healthy, colorful, and bursting with flavor, making it a perfect addition to any meal or gathering. Enjoy this delicious salad as part of your next Mediterranean-inspired feast!

Persian Rice Pilaf

Ingredients:

- 2 cups Basmati rice
- 4 cups water
- 2 tablespoons salt, divided
- 4 tablespoons unsalted butter or ghee, divided
- 1 large onion, thinly sliced
- 1/2 teaspoon ground saffron threads (optional, for coloring and flavor)
- 2 tablespoons plain yogurt (optional, for tahdig)
- Vegetable oil (if needed for tahdig)

Instructions:

Rinse and Soak the Rice:
- Rinse the Basmati rice under cold water until the water runs clear to remove excess starch.
- Place the rinsed rice in a bowl and cover with water. Add 1 tablespoon of salt and let the rice soak for at least 30 minutes.

Parboil the Rice:
- In a large pot, bring 4 cups of water to a boil. Drain the soaked rice and add it to the boiling water.
- Add 1 tablespoon of salt to the water and gently stir.
- Cook the rice for about 6-7 minutes, or until the grains are partially cooked (they should still be firm in the center). Avoid overcooking.

Prepare the Crispy Rice (Tahdig) Base:
- While the rice is parboiling, heat 2 tablespoons of butter (or ghee) in a non-stick pot over medium heat.
- Add the thinly sliced onion to the pot and sauté until golden brown and caramelized, about 10-15 minutes.
- Remove half of the caramelized onions from the pot and set them aside for garnish.

Layer the Rice and Saffron:
- Drain the partially cooked rice and add it to the pot with the remaining caramelized onions.
- Dissolve the ground saffron in 2 tablespoons of hot water. Drizzle the saffron mixture over the rice, distributing it evenly for coloring and flavor.

Create the Tahdig (Crispy Rice Crust):

- In a small bowl, mix the yogurt with a few tablespoons of the parboiling water from the rice.
- Spread the yogurt mixture evenly over the rice in the pot. This will help create a crispy crust (tahdig).
- Melt the remaining 2 tablespoons of butter (or ghee) and drizzle it over the rice.
- Using the handle of a wooden spoon, make several holes in the rice to allow steam to escape and prevent sticking.

Steam the Rice:
- Cover the pot with a clean kitchen towel or paper towel, then place the lid tightly on top to create a seal.
- Reduce the heat to low and steam the rice for about 45-50 minutes, or until the rice is fully cooked and fluffy.

Serve:
- Once the rice is cooked, carefully remove the lid and kitchen towel.
- Gently fluff the rice with a fork to separate the grains.
- Transfer the Persian Rice Pilaf to a serving platter, garnish with the reserved caramelized onions, and serve hot.

Serving Suggestions:

- Serve Persian Rice Pilaf with your favorite Persian stew, such as Ghormeh Sabzi (herb stew) or Fesenjan (pomegranate walnut stew).
- Pair it with grilled kebabs, roasted vegetables, or salad for a complete meal.

Persian Rice Pilaf is a classic dish that requires some technique but yields a delicious and impressive result. The combination of fluffy rice and crispy tahdig is irresistible and makes for a memorable dining experience. Enjoy this flavorful rice pilaf as part of your next Persian feast!

Stuffed Grape Leaves (Dolmas)

Ingredients:

For the Grape Leaves:

- 1 jar of grape leaves in brine (about 60-70 leaves)
- Water, for rinsing and soaking grape leaves

For the Filling:

- 1 cup long-grain white rice, rinsed
- 1/2 lb ground lamb or beef (optional, for a meat version)
- 1 onion, finely chopped
- 2-3 tablespoons pine nuts (optional)
- 2-3 tablespoons currants or chopped raisins (optional)
- 1/4 cup chopped fresh dill
- 1/4 cup chopped fresh parsley
- 1/4 cup chopped fresh mint (optional)
- 1/4 cup lemon juice
- 1/4 cup extra virgin olive oil
- Salt and pepper, to taste

For Cooking:

- Water or broth, as needed
- Lemon slices, for garnish (optional)

Instructions:

Prepare the Grape Leaves:
- Drain the jar of grape leaves and rinse them thoroughly under cold water to remove excess salt.
- Place the grape leaves in a large bowl of warm water and let them soak for 10-15 minutes to soften. This will make them easier to work with.

Make the Filling:
- In a mixing bowl, combine the rinsed rice, ground meat (if using), chopped onion, pine nuts, currants or raisins (if using), chopped fresh herbs (dill, parsley, and mint), lemon juice, and olive oil.
- Season the filling mixture with salt and pepper to taste. Mix well until all ingredients are evenly combined.

Assemble the Dolmas:

- Lay a grape leaf flat on a clean work surface, shiny side down and rib side up.
- Place about 1 tablespoon of the filling near the stem end of the grape leaf (bottom). Fold the sides of the leaf over the filling, then roll it up tightly into a compact cylinder.
- Repeat with the remaining grape leaves and filling mixture until all the filling is used.

Cook the Dolmas:
- In a wide, heavy-bottomed pot, arrange the dolmas in a single layer, seam side down, packing them tightly together.
- Pour enough water or broth over the dolmas to cover them completely. Place a heat-proof plate or lid directly on top of the dolmas to keep them weighted down during cooking.
- Bring the water to a boil over medium-high heat, then reduce the heat to low. Cover the pot and simmer the dolmas for 45-60 minutes, or until the rice is fully cooked and the grape leaves are tender.

Serve:
- Once cooked, carefully remove the dolmas from the pot using a slotted spoon and arrange them on a serving platter.
- Garnish with lemon slices, if desired.

Enjoy:
- Stuffed Grape Leaves (Dolmas) can be served warm or at room temperature as an appetizer or part of a mezze spread. They are delicious with a dollop of yogurt or tzatziki on the side.

Tips:

- If you have leftover filling, you can use it to stuff vegetables like bell peppers or tomatoes.
- Store any leftover dolmas in the refrigerator for up to 3-4 days. They can be enjoyed cold or reheated gently in the microwave or oven before serving.

Stuffed Grape Leaves are a delightful dish that combines savory flavors with tender grape leaves. They are perfect for sharing with family and friends as a part of a festive meal or gathering. Enjoy making and savoring these delicious dolmas!

Honey Roasted Vegetables

Ingredients:

- Assorted vegetables of your choice, such as:
    - Carrots, peeled and cut into sticks
    - Potatoes, peeled and cut into chunks
    - Sweet potatoes, peeled and cut into chunks
    - Bell peppers, sliced
    - Red onion, cut into wedges
    - Zucchini or squash, sliced
    - Brussels sprouts, halved
    - Cauliflower or broccoli florets
- 3 tablespoons olive oil
- 2 tablespoons honey
- 2 cloves garlic, minced
- 1 teaspoon dried thyme (or use fresh thyme leaves)
- Salt and pepper, to taste
- Fresh parsley or thyme leaves, chopped (for garnish)

Instructions:

Preheat the Oven:
- Preheat your oven to 400°F (200°C) and line a baking sheet with parchment paper or foil.

Prepare the Vegetables:
- Wash, peel (if necessary), and chop the vegetables into similar-sized pieces to ensure even cooking.

Make the Honey Glaze:
- In a small bowl, whisk together the olive oil, honey, minced garlic, dried thyme, salt, and pepper until well combined.

Coat the Vegetables:
- Place the chopped vegetables in a large mixing bowl.
- Pour the honey glaze over the vegetables and toss them gently until they are evenly coated with the mixture.

Roast the Vegetables:
- Spread the coated vegetables in a single layer on the prepared baking sheet.

- Roast the vegetables in the preheated oven for about 25-30 minutes, or until they are tender and caramelized, stirring halfway through cooking for even browning.

Serve:
- Once roasted, transfer the honey roasted vegetables to a serving dish.

Garnish and Enjoy:
- Garnish with freshly chopped parsley or thyme leaves for a pop of color and added freshness.

Serve Warm:
- Serve the honey roasted vegetables warm as a delicious side dish with grilled chicken, roasted meats, or as part of a vegetarian meal.

Tips for Variation:

- Feel free to customize this recipe by using your favorite vegetables or what you have on hand.
- Add a sprinkle of red pepper flakes for a touch of heat, if desired.
- Experiment with different herbs such as rosemary or oregano for additional flavor.

Honey Roasted Vegetables are a versatile and flavorful dish that's perfect for any occasion. The sweetness from the honey complements the natural flavors of the vegetables beautifully, making them a favorite among both kids and adults. Enjoy this simple and delicious recipe!

Chocolate Babka

Dough Ingredients:

- 4 cups all-purpose flour
- 1/2 cup granulated sugar
- 1 tablespoon active dry yeast
- 1 teaspoon salt
- 3/4 cup warm milk (about 110°F/43°C)
- 2 large eggs
- 1/2 cup unsalted butter, softened
- 1 teaspoon vanilla extract

Chocolate Filling Ingredients:

- 1 cup semi-sweet chocolate chips or chopped chocolate
- 1/2 cup unsalted butter
- 1/2 cup powdered sugar
- 1/4 cup unsweetened cocoa powder
- 1 teaspoon ground cinnamon (optional)

Syrup Glaze Ingredients:

- 1/4 cup water
- 1/4 cup granulated sugar

Instructions:

Prepare the Dough:
- In a large mixing bowl or the bowl of a stand mixer fitted with a dough hook, combine the flour, sugar, yeast, and salt.
- In a separate bowl, whisk together the warm milk, eggs, softened butter, and vanilla extract.
- Pour the wet ingredients into the dry ingredients and mix until a soft dough forms.
- Knead the dough on a floured surface or using a stand mixer for about 8-10 minutes until smooth and elastic.
- Place the dough in a greased bowl, cover with plastic wrap or a clean kitchen towel, and let it rise in a warm place for 1-2 hours, or until doubled in size.

Make the Chocolate Filling:

- In a heatproof bowl set over a pot of simmering water (or in the microwave), melt together the chocolate chips (or chopped chocolate) and butter until smooth.
- Stir in the powdered sugar, cocoa powder, and ground cinnamon until well combined. Set aside to cool slightly.

Assemble the Babka:
- Punch down the risen dough and divide it in half.
- Roll out each half into a rectangle about 12x16 inches on a floured surface.
- Spread half of the chocolate filling evenly over each rectangle of dough, leaving a small border around the edges.
- Starting from one long edge, tightly roll up each rectangle into a log.
- Use a sharp knife to slice each log in half lengthwise, exposing the layers of filling.
- Twist the two pieces together, keeping the cut sides facing up to expose the filling.
- Carefully transfer the twisted dough into a greased loaf pan or line a baking sheet with parchment paper and form the twisted dough into a wreath shape.

Final Rise and Baking:
- Cover the shaped babka with a clean kitchen towel and let it rise for 30-45 minutes, until puffy.
- Preheat your oven to 350°F (175°C).
- Bake the babka for 30-35 minutes, or until golden brown and cooked through. If the top starts to brown too quickly, tent it with aluminum foil.

Make the Syrup Glaze:
- While the babka is baking, prepare the syrup glaze by combining water and sugar in a small saucepan. Bring to a simmer over medium heat until the sugar dissolves.

Finish and Serve:
- Once baked, remove the babka from the oven and immediately brush the syrup glaze over the top while it's still warm.
- Let the babka cool slightly before slicing and serving. Enjoy your homemade Chocolate Babka with a cup of coffee or tea!

Tips for Variations:

- You can add chopped nuts or raisins to the chocolate filling for extra texture and flavor.

- Experiment with different fillings such as cinnamon sugar, Nutella, or fruit preserves.
- Store leftover babka tightly wrapped at room temperature for up to 3 days, or freeze for longer storage.

Chocolate Babka is a labor of love but well worth the effort for its deliciously sweet and indulgent flavor. Enjoy baking and savoring this classic treat with family and friends!

Coconut Macaroons

Ingredients:

- 3 cups sweetened shredded coconut
- 3/4 cup sweetened condensed milk
- 1 teaspoon vanilla extract
- 2 large egg whites
- 1/4 teaspoon salt
- Optional: 4 ounces semi-sweet or dark chocolate (for dipping)

Instructions:

Preheat the Oven:
- Preheat your oven to 325°F (160°C) and line a baking sheet with parchment paper.

Mix Ingredients:
- In a mixing bowl, combine the sweetened shredded coconut, sweetened condensed milk, and vanilla extract. Stir until well combined.

Whip Egg Whites:
- In a separate clean bowl, whisk the egg whites and salt using a hand mixer or stand mixer until stiff peaks form.

Combine Mixtures:
- Gently fold the whipped egg whites into the coconut mixture using a spatula, until everything is evenly combined and the mixture is sticky.

Shape Macaroons:
- Use a spoon or cookie scoop to portion out the coconut mixture and drop it onto the prepared baking sheet, spacing them about 1 inch apart.
- Optionally, use your hands to shape each portion into a compact mound.

Bake:
- Bake the macaroons in the preheated oven for 20-25 minutes, or until the edges are golden brown and the tops are lightly toasted.

Cool:
- Remove the baking sheet from the oven and let the macaroons cool completely on the pan.

Optional Chocolate Dip:
- If desired, melt the chocolate in a heatproof bowl set over a pot of simmering water (or in the microwave in short bursts, stirring frequently).
- Dip the bottom of each cooled macaroon into the melted chocolate, allowing any excess to drip off.

- Place the dipped macaroons back onto the parchment paper and let the chocolate set at room temperature or in the refrigerator.

Serve and Enjoy:
- Once the chocolate has set (if using), transfer the coconut macaroons to a serving platter.
- Enjoy these delightful coconut treats as a sweet snack or dessert!

Tips for Variation:

- Add chopped nuts (such as almonds or pecans) or dried fruit (such as cranberries or chopped apricots) to the coconut mixture for extra texture and flavor.
- Experiment with different flavors by adding almond extract or lemon zest to the coconut mixture.
- To make the macaroons gluten-free, ensure that all ingredients used are certified gluten-free.

These coconut macaroons are a classic and irresistible treat that's perfect for holidays, parties, or any occasion. They are quick to make and will surely impress with their deliciously sweet coconut flavor. Enjoy making and sharing these delightful cookies!

Israeli Shakshuka

Ingredients:

- 2 tablespoons olive oil
- 1 onion, finely chopped
- 1 red bell pepper, chopped
- 1 yellow bell pepper, chopped
- 3 cloves garlic, minced
- 1 teaspoon ground cumin
- 1 teaspoon paprika
- 1/2 teaspoon chili powder (adjust to taste)
- 1 can (14 oz) diced tomatoes
- Salt and pepper, to taste
- 4-6 eggs
- Fresh parsley or cilantro, chopped (for garnish)
- Crumbled feta cheese (optional, for serving)
- Crusty bread or pita, for serving

Instructions:

Sauté Vegetables:
- Heat the olive oil in a large skillet or cast-iron pan over medium heat.
- Add the chopped onion, red bell pepper, and yellow bell pepper. Sauté for 5-7 minutes until the vegetables start to soften.

Add Spices and Garlic:
- Stir in the minced garlic, ground cumin, paprika, and chili powder. Cook for another minute until the spices are fragrant.

Simmer with Tomatoes:
- Pour in the canned diced tomatoes with their juices. Season with salt and pepper to taste.
- Allow the mixture to simmer over medium heat for 10-15 minutes, stirring occasionally, until the sauce thickens slightly.

Make Wells for Eggs:
- Using a spoon, create small wells or indentations in the tomato-pepper mixture.
- Crack each egg directly into each indentation, taking care not to break the yolks.

Poach the Eggs:

- Cover the skillet with a lid and let the eggs cook over medium-low heat for 7-10 minutes, or until the egg whites are set but the yolks are still runny (cook longer if you prefer firmer yolks).

Garnish and Serve:
- Once the eggs are cooked to your liking, remove the skillet from the heat.
- Garnish the Israeli Shakshuka with chopped fresh parsley or cilantro.
- Optionally, sprinkle crumbled feta cheese over the dish for added flavor.

Serve Warm:
- Serve the Israeli Shakshuka directly from the skillet.
- Enjoy with crusty bread, pita, or your favorite bread for dipping and soaking up the flavorful sauce.

Tips for Variation:

- For a spicier shakshuka, increase the amount of chili powder or add chopped jalapeño peppers.
- Add other vegetables such as zucchini, spinach, or eggplant to the sauce for extra texture and flavor.
- Customize the dish by adding cooked chickpeas, black beans, or diced cooked potatoes for a heartier version.

Israeli Shakshuka is a delicious and satisfying dish that's perfect for sharing with family and friends. It's comforting, flavorful, and easy to prepare, making it a favorite in many households. Enjoy this classic Israeli dish for a tasty meal any time of the day!

Chicken with Preserved Lemons

Ingredients:

- 4 bone-in, skin-on chicken thighs (or other chicken pieces)
- Salt and pepper, to taste
- 2 tablespoons olive oil
- 1 onion, finely chopped
- 3 cloves garlic, minced
- 1 teaspoon ground cumin
- 1 teaspoon ground coriander
- 1/2 teaspoon paprika
- Pinch of saffron threads (optional)
- 1/2 cup chicken broth or water
- 1 preserved lemon, pulp discarded, peel rinsed and thinly sliced
- Fresh cilantro or parsley, chopped, for garnish

Instructions:

Season and Brown the Chicken:
- Season the chicken thighs with salt and pepper on both sides.
- Heat olive oil in a large skillet or Dutch oven over medium-high heat. Add the chicken thighs, skin-side down, and cook for 5-7 minutes until golden brown and crispy. Flip and cook for another 3-4 minutes on the other side. Remove the chicken from the pan and set aside.

Sauté Onion and Spices:
- In the same pan, add the chopped onion and sauté for 3-4 minutes until softened and translucent.
- Add minced garlic, ground cumin, ground coriander, paprika, and saffron threads (if using). Cook for another minute until fragrant.

Simmer with Chicken Broth:
- Pour in the chicken broth or water, scraping the bottom of the pan to deglaze and loosen any browned bits.

Add Preserved Lemons:
- Return the chicken thighs to the pan along with the sliced preserved lemon.

Simmer the Chicken:
- Reduce the heat to low, cover the pan, and let the chicken simmer for 25-30 minutes, or until the chicken is cooked through and tender.

Adjust Seasoning and Serve:

- Taste and adjust the seasoning with salt and pepper if needed.
- Garnish the chicken with chopped fresh cilantro or parsley before serving.

Serving Suggestions:

- Serve the chicken with preserved lemons over cooked couscous, rice, or quinoa.
- Enjoy alongside a salad or steamed vegetables for a complete meal.
- Drizzle any remaining sauce from the pan over the chicken and grains for added flavor.

Tips:

- If you don't have preserved lemons, you can make a quick substitute by using fresh lemon zest and juice to achieve a similar citrusy flavor.
- Feel free to customize the spices based on your preference. Add a pinch of cinnamon or ginger for additional warmth and depth of flavor.

Chicken with preserved lemons is a delicious and aromatic dish that's perfect for dinner parties or special occasions. The tangy and citrusy notes from the preserved lemons complement the savory chicken beautifully, creating a memorable and satisfying meal. Enjoy this flavorful Moroccan-inspired dish!

Yemenite Kubaneh Bread

Ingredients:

- 4 cups all-purpose flour
- 1/4 cup granulated sugar
- 1 teaspoon salt
- 1 packet (2 1/4 teaspoons) active dry yeast
- 1/2 cup warm water
- 1/2 cup unsalted butter, melted
- 1 cup whole milk
- Additional melted butter, for brushing
- Sesame seeds, for garnish (optional)

Instructions:

Prepare the Dough:
- In a large mixing bowl, combine the all-purpose flour, sugar, and salt.
- In a small bowl, dissolve the yeast in warm water and let it sit for 5-10 minutes until foamy.
- Add the melted butter and warm milk to the yeast mixture, then pour this mixture into the dry ingredients.
- Mix everything together to form a dough. Knead the dough on a floured surface for about 8-10 minutes until smooth and elastic.

Let the Dough Rise:
- Place the dough in a greased bowl, cover with plastic wrap or a clean kitchen towel, and let it rise in a warm place for 1-2 hours, or until doubled in size.

Shape the Kubaneh:
- Once the dough has risen, punch it down and divide it into small balls (about 10-12 balls).
- Preheat your oven to 250°F (120°C).
- Take each ball of dough and flatten it slightly with your hands. Brush each flattened dough round generously with melted butter.
- Stack the buttered dough rounds on top of each other to form a tall stack.

Bake the Kubaneh:
- Place the stack of dough rounds in a greased baking dish or a round cake pan.
- Cover the pan tightly with aluminum foil and place it in the preheated oven.

- Bake the Kubaneh at 250°F (120°C) overnight (about 8-10 hours), or until the bread is golden brown, flaky, and cooked through.

Serve:
- Remove the Kubaneh from the oven and let it cool slightly.
- Carefully separate the layers of the flaky bread and serve warm, brushing each piece with additional melted butter if desired.
- Optionally, sprinkle sesame seeds on top for garnish before serving.

Serving Suggestions:

- Serve Yemenite Kubaneh Bread with fresh tomato sauce, grated tomato, or Schug (a spicy Yemenite condiment) for dipping.
- Enjoy Kubaneh with hard-boiled eggs, fresh vegetables, and Israeli salad for a complete breakfast or brunch.

Yemenite Kubaneh Bread is a unique and delicious treat that's worth the effort of slow baking overnight. The flaky layers and buttery richness make it a delightful addition to any special meal or gathering. Enjoy this traditional Yemeni Jewish bread and savor its wonderful flavors!

Date Charoset Truffles

Ingredients:

- 1 cup pitted dates, roughly chopped
- 1/2 cup raisins
- 1/2 cup chopped walnuts or almonds
- 1/2 teaspoon ground cinnamon
- Zest of 1 orange (optional)
- 1 tablespoon sweet red wine or grape juice
- 1 cup dark chocolate chips or chopped dark chocolate
- 1 tablespoon coconut oil

Optional Coatings:

- Finely chopped nuts (e.g., almonds, pistachios)
- Unsweetened cocoa powder
- Toasted coconut flakes

Instructions:

Prepare the Charoset Mixture:
- In a food processor, combine the pitted dates, raisins, chopped nuts, ground cinnamon, orange zest (if using), and sweet red wine or grape juice.
- Process the mixture until it forms a sticky and cohesive paste. You may need to scrape down the sides of the food processor a few times to ensure everything is well combined.

Shape the Truffles:
- Scoop out small portions of the charoset mixture (about 1 tablespoon each) and roll them into balls between your palms. Place the balls on a parchment-lined baking sheet.
- Place the baking sheet in the refrigerator while you prepare the chocolate coating.

Melt the Chocolate:
- In a microwave-safe bowl or using a double boiler, melt the dark chocolate chips or chopped dark chocolate together with the coconut oil until smooth and glossy.

Coat the Truffles:
- Remove the charoset balls from the refrigerator.

- Using a fork or a toothpick, dip each ball into the melted chocolate, allowing any excess chocolate to drip off.
- Place the chocolate-coated truffles back on the parchment-lined baking sheet.

Optional Coatings:
- While the chocolate coating is still wet, you can roll the truffles in finely chopped nuts, unsweetened cocoa powder, or toasted coconut flakes for added flavor and texture.

Chill and Serve:
- Once all the truffles are coated and decorated, place the baking sheet back in the refrigerator for about 15-20 minutes to allow the chocolate to set.
- Once set, transfer the Date Charoset Truffles to an airtight container and store them in the refrigerator until ready to serve.

Serving Suggestions:

- Serve these delicious truffles as a sweet treat during Passover or any special occasion.
- Enjoy alongside other Passover desserts or as a delightful ending to a festive meal.

Date Charoset Truffles are a wonderful way to incorporate the flavors of Passover into a decadent and bite-sized dessert. They are easy to make and can be customized with different coatings to suit your preferences. Enjoy making and sharing these delicious treats with family and friends!

Cheese Burekas

Ingredients:

For the Dough:

- 2 sheets of puff pastry dough, thawed if frozen
- All-purpose flour, for dusting

For the Cheese Filling:

- 1 cup ricotta cheese (or other soft cheese such as feta, farmer's cheese, or a mix)
- 1 cup shredded mozzarella cheese
- 1/4 cup grated Parmesan cheese
- 1 egg, beaten
- 2 tablespoons chopped fresh parsley (optional)
- Salt and pepper, to taste

For Egg Wash (Optional):

- 1 egg, beaten with 1 tablespoon water

Instructions:

Preheat the Oven:
- Preheat your oven to 375°F (190°C) and line a baking sheet with parchment paper.

Prepare the Cheese Filling:
- In a mixing bowl, combine the ricotta cheese, shredded mozzarella cheese, grated Parmesan cheese, beaten egg, chopped parsley (if using), salt, and pepper. Mix well until all ingredients are combined and the mixture is smooth.

Prepare the Dough:
- Lightly dust a clean surface with flour. Roll out one sheet of puff pastry dough into a large rectangle, about 1/8 inch (3 mm) thick.
- Using a knife or pizza cutter, cut the dough into smaller rectangles (about 3x4 inches each).

Assemble the Burekas:
- Place a spoonful of the cheese filling (about 1-2 tablespoons) onto one half of each dough rectangle, leaving a border around the edges.

- Fold the other half of the dough over the filling to enclose it, creating a pocket or turnover shape.
- Use a fork to press down and seal the edges of each bureka. Repeat with the remaining dough and filling.

Optional Egg Wash:
- If desired, brush the tops of the burekas with the beaten egg wash. This will give them a shiny golden finish when baked.

Bake the Burekas:
- Place the assembled burekas on the prepared baking sheet, spacing them a few inches apart.
- Bake in the preheated oven for 20-25 minutes, or until the burekas are puffed up and golden brown.

Serve Warm:
- Remove the cheese burekas from the oven and let them cool slightly on the baking sheet.
- Serve the cheese burekas warm as a delicious appetizer or snack.

Tips for Variation:

- Add additional herbs or spices to the cheese filling for extra flavor, such as chopped dill, oregano, or garlic powder.
- Experiment with different types of cheese for the filling, such as feta cheese, farmer's cheese, or a combination of your favorite cheeses.
- Serve cheese burekas with a side of marinara sauce, tzatziki, or hummus for dipping.

Cheese burekas are a delightful savory pastry that's easy to make and perfect for sharing. They can be enjoyed warm or at room temperature, making them a versatile and crowd-pleasing appetizer. Enjoy making these cheese-filled treats at home and savoring their delicious flavors!

Beet Salad with Goat Cheese

Ingredients:

- 3-4 medium-sized beets, preferably a mix of red and golden beets
- 4 oz (about 113g) goat cheese, crumbled
- Mixed greens (such as arugula, baby spinach, or spring mix)
- 1/4 cup chopped walnuts or pecans, toasted (optional)
- Fresh herbs (such as parsley or chives), chopped (for garnish)

For the Vinaigrette:

- 3 tablespoons extra virgin olive oil
- 1 tablespoon balsamic vinegar (or red wine vinegar)
- 1 teaspoon Dijon mustard
- Salt and pepper, to taste

Instructions:

Roast the Beets:
- Preheat your oven to 400°F (200°C).
- Wash and trim the beets, then wrap each beet individually in aluminum foil. Place the wrapped beets on a baking sheet.
- Roast the beets in the preheated oven for about 45-60 minutes, or until they are tender when pierced with a fork. The roasting time will vary depending on the size of the beets.
- Once roasted, remove the beets from the oven and let them cool slightly. Use a paper towel to rub off the skin, which should come off easily.
- Cut the roasted beets into wedges or cubes and set aside.

Prepare the Vinaigrette:
- In a small bowl, whisk together the olive oil, balsamic vinegar, Dijon mustard, salt, and pepper until well combined. Adjust seasoning to taste.

Assemble the Salad:
- In a large salad bowl, combine the mixed greens with the roasted beet wedges or cubes.
- Drizzle the vinaigrette over the salad and toss gently to coat the greens and beets evenly.

Add Goat Cheese and Nuts:
- Sprinkle the crumbled goat cheese over the salad.
- If using, scatter the toasted chopped walnuts or pecans on top.

Garnish and Serve:

- Garnish the beet salad with chopped fresh herbs, such as parsley or chives.
- Serve the salad immediately as a side dish or light meal.

Tips for Variation:

- For added sweetness, you can roast the beets with a drizzle of honey or maple syrup.
- Substitute the goat cheese with feta cheese or blue cheese for a different flavor profile.
- Add sliced red onions or thinly sliced apples or pears to the salad for extra texture and flavor contrast.
- If you prefer a more substantial salad, you can add cooked quinoa or farro to make it a hearty main course.

Beet salad with goat cheese is a delightful combination of flavors and textures that's perfect for any occasion. It's easy to prepare and makes a stunning addition to your table. Enjoy this delicious and nutritious salad with the sweet earthiness of roasted beets and creamy goat cheese!

Apple Kugel

Ingredients:

- 8 oz (about 225g) wide egg noodles
- 4-5 medium apples (such as Granny Smith or Honeycrisp), peeled, cored, and thinly sliced
- 1/2 cup granulated sugar
- 1 teaspoon ground cinnamon
- 1/2 cup raisins (optional)
- 4 large eggs
- 1 cup sour cream
- 1/2 cup unsalted butter, melted
- 1 teaspoon vanilla extract
- Pinch of salt
- Additional cinnamon-sugar mixture for sprinkling on top

Instructions:

Preheat the Oven:
- Preheat your oven to 350°F (175°C). Grease a 9x13-inch baking dish with butter or cooking spray.

Cook the Noodles:
- Cook the egg noodles according to the package instructions until they are al dente. Drain and set aside.

Prepare the Apple Mixture:
- In a large bowl, combine the sliced apples, granulated sugar, ground cinnamon, and raisins (if using). Toss well to coat the apples evenly with the sugar and spices.

Make the Custard Mixture:
- In another bowl, whisk together the eggs, sour cream, melted butter, vanilla extract, and a pinch of salt until smooth and well combined.

Assemble the Kugel:
- In the prepared baking dish, layer half of the cooked noodles on the bottom.
- Spread half of the apple mixture over the noodles.
- Repeat with another layer of the remaining noodles and top with the rest of the apple mixture.

Pour the Custard Over:

- Pour the custard mixture evenly over the noodles and apples in the baking dish. Use a spoon or spatula to gently press down the mixture to ensure the noodles are coated.

Bake the Kugel:
- Sprinkle the top of the kugel with a cinnamon-sugar mixture for added flavor and a golden crust.
- Bake in the preheated oven for 45-50 minutes, or until the kugel is set and golden brown on top.

Serve Warm:
- Remove the apple kugel from the oven and let it cool slightly before serving.
- Cut into squares or scoops and serve warm as a delicious side dish or dessert.

Tips for Variation:

- Add chopped nuts (such as walnuts or pecans) to the apple mixture for added crunch and texture.
- Substitute part of the sour cream with cottage cheese or Greek yogurt for a lighter version of the kugel.
- Experiment with different spices such as nutmeg or cardamom for a unique flavor profile.

Apple kugel is a comforting and satisfying dish that's perfect for fall gatherings or holiday meals. The combination of sweet apples, warm spices, and creamy custard makes it a delightful treat that everyone will enjoy. Serve this delicious apple kugel alongside your favorite main dishes for a memorable meal!

Turkish Coffee

Ingredients:

- Freshly ground Turkish coffee (finely ground, similar to espresso grind)
- Cold water
- Sugar (optional)

Equipment Needed:

- Turkish coffee pot (cezve or ibrik)
- Small coffee cups (traditionally small and handle-less)

Instructions:

Measure the Ingredients:
- For each cup of Turkish coffee, use about 1 heaping tablespoon (or 5-6 grams) of finely ground coffee.

Add Water and Sugar (if desired):
- Measure cold water using the same coffee cup you will be serving in. Add water to the cezve (Turkish coffee pot) based on the number of cups you are making.
- Optionally, add sugar to taste. Traditionally, Turkish coffee is served unsweetened ("sade"), with a little sugar ("az şekerli"), or sweet ("şekerli"). A common guideline is 1-2 teaspoons of sugar per cup, but you can adjust based on your preference.

Mix and Heat:
- Stir the water and sugar (if using) in the cezve until the sugar dissolves.

Add Coffee:
- Add the finely ground coffee to the cezve. Do not stir after adding the coffee.

Brewing:
- Place the cezve over low heat (or medium-low heat, depending on your stove) and slowly bring it to a simmer. Be patient and avoid boiling the coffee too quickly.
- As the coffee heats up, a foam will start to form on the surface. Allow this foam to rise without letting it boil over.

Pour and Serve:

- Once the coffee begins to froth and the foam rises, remove the cezve from the heat. Carefully pour the coffee into the small coffee cups, ensuring that each cup gets some of the foam.
- Let the coffee sit for a minute or two to allow the grounds to settle at the bottom of the cup.

Enjoy:
- Turkish coffee is traditionally sipped slowly, allowing the rich flavors to be savored. Take small sips and enjoy the experience!

Serving Suggestions:

- Turkish coffee is often served with a glass of water to cleanse the palate between sips.
- It pairs well with Turkish delight or other sweet treats.

Tips:

- The key to making good Turkish coffee is controlling the heat. You want to bring the coffee to a gentle simmer without boiling it rapidly.
- Adjust the sweetness and strength of the coffee based on your personal preference. Start with less sugar if you're unsure and add more to taste.
- Turkish coffee is meant to be strong and thick, with a layer of sediment at the bottom of the cup. Do not stir the coffee after pouring, as the grounds should settle naturally.

Enjoy the rich and aromatic experience of Turkish coffee, a timeless tradition that brings people together over a cup of finely brewed coffee.

Fruit Compote

Ingredients:

- 4 cups of mixed fresh or frozen fruits (such as berries, peaches, apples, pears, plums, or cherries), washed, peeled, pitted, and sliced as needed
- 1/4 cup granulated sugar (adjust based on the sweetness of the fruits)
- 1/2 cup water
- 1 tablespoon lemon juice (optional, for acidity and flavor)
- 1 teaspoon vanilla extract (optional, for added flavor)

Instructions:

Prepare the Fruits:
- Wash, peel (if necessary), pit, and slice the fruits as needed. You can use a variety of fruits based on your preference and what's in season.

Make the Sugar Syrup:
- In a saucepan, combine the granulated sugar and water. Bring the mixture to a simmer over medium heat, stirring occasionally until the sugar is completely dissolved.

Add the Fruits:
- Once the sugar syrup is ready, add the prepared fruits to the saucepan.

Simmer the Compote:
- Bring the mixture to a gentle simmer. Reduce the heat to low and let the fruits simmer for about 10-15 minutes, or until the fruits are tender and the syrup has thickened slightly.

Add Lemon Juice and Vanilla Extract:
- Stir in the lemon juice and vanilla extract (if using). These additions will brighten the flavors of the compote.

Cool and Serve:
- Remove the saucepan from the heat and let the fruit compote cool slightly.
- You can serve the fruit compote warm, at room temperature, or chilled, depending on your preference.

Store the Compote:
- Transfer the fruit compote to a clean jar or airtight container. Allow it to cool completely before refrigerating.
- Fruit compote can be stored in the refrigerator for up to a week. It can also be frozen for longer storage.

Serving Suggestions:

- Serve the fruit compote as a topping for pancakes, waffles, French toast, oatmeal, or yogurt.
- Enjoy the fruit compote on its own as a light and refreshing dessert.
- Use the fruit compote as a filling for pies, tarts, or turnovers.
- Drizzle the fruit compote over ice cream or pound cake for a simple and elegant dessert.

Tips:

- Adjust the sweetness of the compote based on the natural sweetness of the fruits. Taste the syrup before adding the fruits and adjust the sugar accordingly.
- Feel free to customize the flavors by adding spices such as cinnamon, ginger, or cloves to the sugar syrup.
- Experiment with different combinations of fruits and flavors to create your own unique fruit compote recipe.

Fruit compote is a delightful way to enjoy seasonal fruits and can be prepared quickly with minimal ingredients. It's a versatile and satisfying dish that's perfect for breakfast, brunch, or dessert. Enjoy making and savoring this delicious fruit compote!

www.ingramcontent.com/pod-product-compliance
Lightning Source LLC
LaVergne TN
LVHW061939070526
838199LV00060B/3880